INSIGHT GUIDES

EXPLORE
BARCELONA

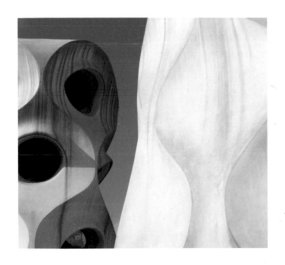

CONTENTS

ARCHITECTURE

From pure Catalan Gothic around the Royal Palace (route 2) to the Modernista showcases of the Eixample (route 10), including Barcelona's greatest work-in-progress, the Sagrada Família (route 11).

RECOMMENDED ROUTES FOR...

ART BUFFS

Artistic highlights include the Museu Picasso (route 5) and Montjuïc's Fundacío Miró and Palau Nacional, home to the world's best collection of Romanesque art (route 12). Dalí fans must make a trip to Figueres (route 19).

FAMILIES WITH KIDS

Kids will enjoy the Wax Museum (route 1), the boating lake in Parc de la Ciutadella (route 8), the beach (route 9), Barça football club (route 13) and CosmoCaixa science museum and Tibidabo funfair (route 16).

FLORA AND FAUNA

For a spot of greenery, to look for parakeets, or to check out the zoo, visit the Parc de la Ciutadella (route 8). Horticultural lovers should head for the various gardens on hilly Montjuïc (route 12).

FOOD AND DRINK

Sample the excellent tapas on and around the Passeig de Gràcia (route 10) or slip up to Gràcia (route 15) for a drink in one of the authentic local bars. Excursions include a tour of Catalonia's wine region (route 18).

MUSIC LOVERS

El Liceu opera house (route 1) and the gorgeous Modernista Palau de la Música Catalana (route 4) should be top of your list. Also recommended is the wonderful music museum, the Museu de la Música (route 8).

NIGHT OWLS

You will find places that open late across the city, but good starting points include El Born (route 5) and La Rambla (route 1), which is busy day and night. Or chill out by the waterfront at Port Olímpic (route 9).

SPORTY TYPES

Visit the buildings erected for the 1992 Olympics and check out the Museu Olímpic i de l'Esport at Montjuïc (route 12) or pay homage to Barça football club at Camp Nou (route 13).

INTRODUCTION

An introduction to Barcelona's geography, customs and culture, plus illuminating background information on cuisine, history and what to do when you're there.

The view from Park Güell

EXPLORE BARCELONA

A vibrant, dynamic city, always on the move but passionately guarding its heritage, Barcelona offers everything from Gothic treasures and traditional dances to trendy bars, innovative architecture and gorgeous food.

When anyone asks what are the best things to see in Barcelona, the answer should always be: just walk the streets. Few cities in the world are so agreeable for simply wandering, thanks to Barcelona's rich architectural heritage, from giant Roman stones and sunless medieval lanes to the brilliant architecture of Gaudí and the Modernistas, and the shimmering, sharp-edged 21st-century blocks that are placed with such panache alongside the historical gems.

DEVELOPMENT

Lying on the Mediterranean coast in northeast Spain, some 260km (160 miles) from France and a distance of 625km (390 miles) from Madrid, Spain's second-largest city was founded by the Romans. The *oppidum* of Barcino was entrenched behind walls encircling the area around what is now the cathedral and the government buildings of Plaça de Sant Jaume. During medieval times – Catalonia's Golden Age – the Counts of Barcelona pushed the walls south beyond the famous La Rambla avenue, to encom-

pass El Raval and create what is now the whole of the old town, or Ciutat Vella. Beyond this lay the hillside Jewish burial grounds of Montjuïc.

The 19th century

Towards the end of the 19th century a vast new extension (Eixample) was laid out in an impeccable grid system inland, while an industrial area spread north alongside the shore. The Ciutat Vella, the Eixample (where Antoni Gaudí's Sagrada Família and many of the Modernista showcase buildings are located) and the former industrial area that has been transformed into a beach front (Barceloneta and the port) are the three key areas that most visitors come to explore.

NAVIGATING THE CITY

Centred on the Plaça de Catalunya that separates the old part of town from the new, Barcelona is an easy city to navigate. The grid system of the Eixample is simple to follow, and though the lanes of the Ciutat Vella are more maze like, that is half the fun. A good way to get to know your way around is

Strolling down the Rambla *Popular Barceloneta Beach*

to take a ride on the tourist bus, which passes all the main sights, where you can hop on and off. Taking a trip around the port in a Golondrina pleasure boat is another way to get a sense of the city, while cable cars and funiculars whisk you up to its high spots for bird's-eye views.

If you head up to the castle at the top of Montjuïc, you can see the city stretching far to the south, beyond the commercial port, down to the Llobregat River. In the other direction, heading north, if you walk the whole length of the beach you will eventually arrive at the new Forum and the River Bésos, marking the city's northern edge. The Serra Collserola, with Tibidabo's Sagrat Cor church pricking the sky-

line, stops the city from expanding far inland.

Public transport

The transport system, including a highly efficient metro network, is straightforward to navigate. Metro, rail and bus services are all paid for using the same tickets, which are comparatively inexpensive, especially if you buy them in blocks of 10. For more information on this, consult the Directory chapter (see page 130).

Correfoc festival in full swing

Festivals and partying

The Barcelonans like to party, and barely a month goes by without some excuse for a celebration. Each district's *festa major* (main festival) involves large family meals, dishes and pastries created specially for the occasion, plus crates of cava and lots of music. The city's principal festival is the week-long La Mercè in September, with spectacular parades of 'giants', 'dragons' and 'devils' with music and dance and fireworks. In addition to this the festive calendar is marked with celebrations at Carnival, just before Lent, and the eve of the Feast of St John, on 23 June. Two peculiarly Catalan contributions to the party scene are the traditional *sardana* dance (see page 39) and *castells*, human 'towers' that reach five people high. More tranquil is the celebration of St George, patron of Catalonia, when red roses and books are given as gifts.

Skateboarders in Parc Diagonal Mar

THE BARRIOS

In spite of the city's size, the communities and villages that make up Barcelona give it an intimate feel. These *barrios* (districts) have strong identities and flavours, celebrating their own festivals and making their own entertainment, for example. Usually centred on a square or two, where the outdoor seating that is common in Barcelona allows people to stop for a chat, these *barrios* maintain their individuality. And with a mild climate and temperatures rarely falling below 10°C (50°F) in winter, and rising to 25°C (77°F) in summer, it is not surprising that people spend much of their time outdoors. Wherever you stay in the city, you are soon likely to find a favourite street or

DON'T LEAVE BARCELONA WITHOUT...

Doing a tapas crawl. From the tiny, more traditional bars to the more contemporary and fusion: there is a tapas bar to please everyone. See our recommendations throughout the book and on page 15.

Seeing Gaudí art. You won't be able to avoid him even if you want to: from his imposing Sagrada Família and Park Güell, to the more intimate La Pedrera or Casa Batlló. See pages 68 and 72.

Walking the Modernista Route. Purchase a copy of the Ruta del Modernisme guide in one of the three Modernisme centres, tourist outlets and some bookshops for the low-down on all 115 identified sites in the city and beyond, including restaurants and bars, with discount vouchers (www.rutadel modernisme.com). See page 22.

Treating yourself to a *orxata*. The Barri Gòtic is known for its *granges* (or *granjas*), literally 'dairies'. These traditional cafés sell mainly milk-based drinks, including *orxata*, a thick beverage made with milk and tiger nuts. *Granges* usually also have a good selection of pastries. See page 67.

Having breakfast at La Boqueria. La Boqueria market is at its most colourful in the morning. Indulge in a proper Catalan breakfast like baby squid and poached eggs at El Quim de la Boqueria. See page 32.

Ambling the narrow streets of the Gothic Quarter. Meander through its shady narrow lanes and palm-filled courtyards. Get the background on today's Old Town at the City History Museum or break for coffee in the diminutive Meson del Café on Llibreteria. See page 36.

Dancing the *sardana* on Sunday. Toes tapping? Meet up with locals outside the cathedral on a Sunday morning to do the *sardana*, Catalonia's traditional dance. See page 39.

Admiring the view from Montjuïc. Tour 12 takes you up the hilly Montjuïc to admire the legacy of the 1992 Olympic Games. Only the brave dare to jump from the highest diving board in the city, but everyone can admire the views. See page 75.

Taking it easy in El Raval

Watching the world go by

square with a bar or café where regulars gather for a morning *cortado* (coffee) or lunch-time ice cream. And you will soon find yourself slipping into the rhythm of late starts (shops open around 10am), quiet afternoons and buzzing early evenings, when everyone seems to be out and about for a stroll in the city's streets.

STRONG HERITAGE

Like the city's numerous long-established cafés and bars, many shops seem

The lipstick-shaped Torre Agbar

rooted in the past. It is hard to think of a major city that maintains so many specialist shops: a *pollería* selling nothing but chicken; a *cuchillería* selling knives, a *colmado* that stocks only dried goods. The influx of immigrants has only added to this mix. The city's commercial individuality is borne out, too, with the modern boutiques and one-off designer outlets of El Raval and El Born, where small premises are often just a workshop with a window.

CREATIVE SPIRIT

Diseny (design) is the most pervasive talent in a city that has produced some explosive creativity, in both the plastic and performing arts. The national characteristic is said to be a mix of *seny* (wisdom) and *rauxa* – a kind of wildness that produces creativity. It results in a mix of deep conservatism and mercurial flair, which might explain the Sagrada Família, an extraordinary avant-garde work by a deeply religious traditionalist. It perhaps also explains the city's history, a mix of highs and lows, of times of great prosperity and times of gruelling hardship, times of enlightened thinking and times of incendiary passion.

URBAN PLANNING

The city's urban planning is a match for its architectural bravura. Barcelona is a city whose planners take bold

Café life on Plaça de Pau Vila

steps, in spite of frequent opposition. They are unafraid to pull down great chunks of old properties and replace them with cutting-edge modern buildings, or simply leave breathing spaces.

Growth spurts

The city has grown in bursts: the Golden Age of the 13th and 14th centuries produced the Gothic mansions of the Ciutat Vella. Architectural development was low-key until the 19th-century industrial boom funded the Modernista extravaganza of the Eixample, under the supervision of engineer Ildefons Cerdà.

In the mid-20th century, however, the fascist dictator General Franco put a stop to just about everything. In the second half of the 20th century, while other European cities were ripping out their architectural heritage and throwing up skyscrapers, Barcelona languished, unloved by the holders of the national purse strings.

It was not until 1986 and the prospect of the Olympic Games that the city reawakened, attracting architects of the highest calibre in a second *Renaixença* (Renaissance).

A dynamic city

After years of stagnation and recession, the city is on the move again, with world-famous architects like Calatrava, Foster and Rogers clamouring to put their buildings here. The focus is on the two main arteries running east–west to the sea, Avinguda Diagonal and Avinguda Paral.lel, creating a cohesive connection to the port with its cruise-ship terminal, and the Forum's trade fair, exhibition and conference venues. The former industrial area, Poble Nou, has either been cleared or had its factories converted to make way for a high-tech explosion. Supporting all this are new transport links, both over and underground. Debate rages as to whether this will destroy the authentic spirit of Barcelona or happily co-exist with its industrial heritage.

Barcelonans love their ice cream

La Rambla at dusk   *Torre Mare Nostrum on Avinguda Diagonal*

TOP TIPS FOR EXPLORING BARCELONA

Late habits. Everything starts late in Barcelona: lunch is not usually until 2pm and dinner not until at least 9pm or 10pm, which is when most concerts start. Live-music venues and clubs do not get going until 2am. Pace yourself with a few tapas.

Shopping hours. The vast majority of shops open between 9am and 10am and close for lunch between 1 and 2pm, opening again between 4 and 5pm until 8pm. Many clothes and food shops close at 8.30 or 9pm. The large department stores, chain stores and shopping galleries remain open through lunch time. In the summer smaller shops may close on Saturday afternoon. Only bakeries, pastry shops and a few groceries are open on Sunday (until around 3pm). Most food markets open daily except Sunday from early morning until around 3pm.

Bargain hunting. Every Thursday there is an antiques and bric-a-brac market in Plaça Nova outside the cathedral (10am–9pm, closed three to four weeks in August and early September).

Helicopter ride. Cat Helicòpters (www.cat helicopters.com) offers 10-minute flights over the city, covering the Olympic sites, Barça football stadium, Tibidabo, Park Güell, the Sagrada Família, the Fòrum and port. The heliport is located at Moll Adossat, the cruise-ship quay.

Fashion tips. Some of Barcelona's key designers are based in the Eixample. One of the best known is Antonio Miró, whose shop is at Carrer del Consell de Cent 349. Other places to visit include Adolfo Dominguez (Passeig de Gràcia 32) and On Land (Carrer de Princesa 25), the latter with clothes for both men and women from young and established designers. Camiseria Pons is attractively located in a Modernista building at Carrer Gran de Gràcia 49. Salvador Bachiller (Carrer de Mallorca 243) has been creating accessories and travel goods since 1942 but is still on trend.

Barça ticket sales. Match tickets can be purchased in advance online through the club's website. Same-day tickets can be bought in the stadium's ticket offices on Travessera de les Corts or Avinguda de Joan XXIII. Matches start between 5 and 9pm. Entrada general are cheap, top-tier tickets, Lateral are mid-priced ones, and Tribuna are for covered seats. Note that tickets are scarce for big matches.

CosmoCaixa. Be warned that the entrance fee to the science museum is higher than that for most Barcelona museums. This reflects the wear and tear that the interactive machines suffer from parties of eager schoolchildren.

Wine tours. There are travel agencies and tour operators that organise wine and gastronomy tours from Barcelona. The most comprehensive information on visits to some 300 wine and cava producers can be found at the Vilafranca Tourist Office (Carrer Cort 14; tel: 93 892 03 58; www.turismevilafranca.com).

Jamón–carving is an artform

FOOD AND DRINK

Barcelonans are serious about their food. 'Where did you eat?' they will ask with interest, and your reply will mark you out either as a person of taste and distinction or as someone who needs taking in hand.

Catalan cuisine is an ancient Mediterranean style of cooking, characterised by the aromas of mountain herbs, the oils and the juices of the plains, the wild meat of the woods and skies, and the flesh of the fish and crustaceans of the sea. *Mar i muntanya* (sea and mountain) is how it is described, a special mixture of seafood and meat. In recent years the trend has been towards a more avant-garde approach to the Catalan classics, inspired by Michelin-starred chefs. However, a new breed of chefs is increasingly turning back to a simpler style and the use of local, seasonal ingredients is paramount.

Many other cuisines can be tried in Barcelona, and there is certainly no shortage of places to eat. The smarter restaurants in the Eixample may have some of the best food, but they tend to lack the personality of restaurants in the Old Town, where classic establishments such as Agut, Caracoles and 7 Portes increasingly rub shoulders with newer, trendier places.

Most bars (or *tabernas*, *bodegas* and *cervecerías*, the last meaning 'beer hall') also serve food, often of a surprisingly high standard. Here you can sample tapas, sandwiches (*bocadillos* in Castilian, *bocats* or *entrepans* in Catalan) or *plats combinats* (single-course meals) at almost any time of the day.

Fresh produce at La Boqueria

MAIN MEALS

Local people usually have an early breakfast of *café con leche* (milky coffee, *cafè amb llet* in Catalan) accompanied by toast or biscuits. Around 11am it is time for a second breakfast, which tends to be a more substantial sand-

Tempting tapas   *Xurros and chocolate*

wich or chunky wedge of potato omelette, or pastries.

Late lunch, late dinner

At other meal times, Barcelonans, like all
Spaniards, eat late. Lunch usually is not
eaten until 2 or 3pm. Dinner is served
from about 9pm until 11.30pm, although
at weekends people sometimes do not
sit down to dinner until midnight. To last
between lunch and dinner, do as local
people do and fill up on sandwiches
and cakes in the patisseries at around
5.30pm, or tapas in the bars from 7pm.

COURSES AND FIXED-PRICE MENUS

Barcelonans often eat a three-course
meal, including dessert and coffee, at
both lunch and dinner. However, it is not
uncommon to share a first course, or to
order *un sólo plato* – just a main course.
Many restaurants offer a lunch time
menú del día or *menú de la casa*, a daily
set menu that generally offers excellent
value for money. For a fixed price you
will get three courses: a starter, often
soup or salad, a main dish, and dessert (ice cream, a piece of fruit or the
ubiquitous *flan* (*flam* in Catalan), a kind
of caramel custard), plus wine, beer or
bottled water, and bread. Typically, the
cost is about half of what you would
expect to pay if you ordered the same
dishes à la carte. Many Spaniards order
the *menú*, so there is no need to think
you are getting the 'tourist special'.

What to eat

A typical dinner might begin with *ama-
nida catalana*, a salad with cold meats;
or *escalivada*, baked peppers and
aubergines, skinned, covered in oil and
eaten cold; or *esqueixada*, a salad with
shredded cod. A main course could be
suquet (fish stew) or *estofat* (meat stew),
botifarra amb mongetes (sausage and
beans), or rabbit *(conill)*, served with
snails *(cargols)* or a garlicky alioli sauce.
Although it originates in rice-growing
Valencia, the classic seafood dish of
paella is high on many visitors' lists of
dishes to sample in Barcelona. Try the
restaurants in Barceloneta for a paella
of fresh mussels, clams, shrimp and
several kinds of fish. It will take about
20 minutes to prepare. Another delicacy
is *fideuá*, which is similar to paella but
made with noodles instead of rice.

When it comes to dessert, *crema catalana* (egg custard with caramelised
sugar on top) is a highlight. *Mel i mato*
is another treat, made with honey and
creamy cheese. The best sweets are generally the delicacies sold in pastry shops.

TAPAS AND RACIONES

Tapas (*tapes* in Catalan) – the snacks
for which Spanish bars and cafés are
world-famous – come in dozens of delicious varieties, from appetisers such as
olives and salted almonds, to vegetable
salads, fried squid, garlicky shrimps, lob-
ster mayonnaise, meatballs, spiced potatoes, wedges of omelette, sliced sausage

Fish restaurant in the port

and cheese. The list is endless, and can be surprisingly creative, especially at the now extremely popular Basque tapas joints, where they are called *pintxos*.

A dish larger than a *tapa* is called a *porción*. A complete serving, meant to be shared, is a *ración*, and half of this, a *media ración*. Tapas are usually available throughout the day, and provide a great way to sample new dishes.

Chocolate

If you like chocolate, you are in the right place. You can drink *xocolata desfeta*, chocolate thick enough to stand a spoon up in (great for dipping *xurros* into), see fantastic festive creations and eat unusual dishes such as chocolate with rabbit or squid – apparently a traditional combination. Well-established chocolate makers include the Escribà family, with a shop on La Rambla (No. 83), and elsewhere you can find it in raw, brick-sized lumps. New and inventive chocolate makers are moving in. Try Cacao Sampaka's handmade bars, sauces and creams (Carrer Consell de Cent 292 or Carrer Laforja 96). Or taste chocolate beer and buy chocolate candles at Xocoa (Carrer Petrixol 11; www.xocoa-bcn.com). At Plaça Sant Gregori Taumaturg, you'll find award-winning Oriol Balaguer (www.oriolbalaguer.com). And to find out how it all started, visit the Museu de la Xocolata (Chocolate Museum, Carrer del Commerç 36; www.museuxocolata.cat).

They can also be filling, especially when eaten with *pa amb tomàquet*, bread rubbed with garlic, olive oil and tomato. This bread works well with ham *(pernil)*, spicy sausage *(xoriço)*, cheese *(formatge)* or anchovies *(anxoves)*.

Other dishes to point to on the bar might be *truites* (*tortillas* in Spanish: omelettes made with potato and onion, and sometimes also with spinach); small fried fish; octopus; snails; or *patates braves*, potatoes in a hot tomato sauce.

MICHELIN STARS

In 2013 the number of Michelin-starred restaurants in Barcelona and its immediate environs stood at 19, with four restaurants having two stars: Abac, headed by sensational young chef Jodi Cruz, Lasarte, Enoteca and Moments. The other 16 have one star each. The majority of these restaurants are in luxury hotels in the Eixample district. Since the closure of world-renowned El Bulli in 2011, there remain just two three-starred restaurants in Catalonia: Sant Pau and El Celler de Can Roca. The influence of El Bulli chef Ferran Adrià has been immense; his approach to cooking has seen a fleet of new chefs bringing an avant-garde technique to their dishes. There has, however, been a trend to return to traditional cooking using high quality and seasonal produce, especially from chefs such as Carme Ruscalleda of the three-starred Sant Pau. This is highlighted in her more recent restaurant,

Dim lighting at Rita Rouge

Be sure to sample the local wines

two-star Moments in Eixample, where her son Raül Balam is head chef.

DRINKS

Wine, cava and beers

Wine is a constant at the Catalan table. In addition to a wide range of fine wines from across Spain, including Rioja, Navarra and Ribera del Duero, Barcelona has some great regional wines. Those from Penedès, the region outside Barcelona where cava, Spain's sparkling wine, is produced, are superb (see page 94). Cava itself goes wonderfully with seafood and tapas. Among Penedès reds, try Torres Gran Coronas, Raimat and Jean León.

Wines from the Priorat area, around an hour to the south of Barcelona (near Tarragona), are superb, robust, expensive reds that rival the best in Spain. Do not be surprised to be offered red wine

Chocolate emporium Xocoa.

(*vi negre*) chilled in hot weather. There are also several delicious, dry rosés (*vi rosat*) from the region.

Spanish beers, which are available in bottles and on draft, are generally light and refreshing.

Other alcoholic drinks

Sangría, made of wine and fruit fortified with brandy, is drunk mostly by visitors. Locals favour sherry (*jerez*), of which you will find every kind here. Pale, dry *fino* is drunk as an aperitif but also with soup and fish courses. Rich dark *oloroso* goes well after dinner. Brandy is another option as a *digestif*: Spanish brandy varies from excellent to rough: you get what you pay for. Other spirits are made under licence in Spain, and are usually cheap.

Hot drinks

Coffee is typically served black (*solo*), with a spot of milk (*cortado/tallat*), or half and half with hot milk (*con leche/ amb llet*). *Orxata*, made with ground tiger nuts and milk, is also popular, and is served both hot and cold.

Food and Drink Prices

Throughout this book, price guide for a three-course à la carte dinner for one with a bottle of house wine:
€€€€ = over 60 euros
€€€ = 40–60 euros
€€= 25–40 euros
€ = below 25 euros

Shoes are great value

SHOPPING

Barcelona is a great place to shop, from its innovative, design-conscious showcases around the Passeig de Gràcia and Diagonal to the timeless independent shops in the Barri Gòtic and cutting-edge boutiques in El Born.

In keeping with its reputation as a centre for style and design, Barcelona has an impressive range of fashion boutiques, antiques shops, state-of-the-art home interior stores and art galleries. Shopping is extremely pleasant here, as the city has not been totally overtaken by homogenous chain stores and still has many quirky and enticing family-owned shops. The best items to buy include trendy clothing, shoes and other leather products, antiques, books (Barcelona is the publishing capital of Spain), high-tech design and home furnishings.

SHOPPING AREAS

The Passeig de Gràcia, Rambla de Catalunya and interconnecting streets are good for chain stores, high-end fashions and boutiques. The same goes for the Barri Gòtic, which also has many artisanal shops, galleries and trendy souvenir sellers, plus hip clothes stores as you move towards El Born. The Avinguda Diagonal, from the top of Rambla de Catalunya to the roundabout that forms Plaça Francesc Macià, and the streets behind, are good for fashion at the top end of the market, while Gràcia is a relaxed place to shop, with cutting-edge young designer fashion and jewellery. The Arenas de Barcelona complex, in the old bullring building in Plaça d'Espanya, which opened in 2011, has a good range of popular brands and speciality shops.

DEPARTMENT STORES

The largest department store in Barcelona is El Corte Inglés, with a branch in Plaça de Catalunya, another in nearby Portal de l'Angel specialising in leisure, music, books and sports, and others in Avinguda Diagonal. All branches are open Monday to Saturday, from 9.30am till 9.30pm. The branches on the Plaça de Catalunya and Diagonal (No. 617) have excellent supermarkets.

FASHION

Designer clothes
Antonio Miró (no relation to the artist) is perhaps the most famous Catalan designer of men's- and women's-wear, with clothes characterised by low-key

Bright colours at Antonio Miró　　　　　　　　*Historic hat shop in the Barri Gòtic*

design and clean lines. His shop can be found at Carrer del Consell de Cent 349. Other designer names to look for include Adolfo Dominguez, David Valls, Jean Pierre Bua, Josep Abril and Kristia Robustella. An iconic Catalan name in the world of fashion is the dynamic Custo-Barcelona, whose flagship store is located in the shopping mall at Avinguda Diagonal 557.

High-street fashion

In the old town, Carrer de la Portaferrissa and Portal de l'Angel are good for young fashion stores. On and around Carrer d'Avinyó there are lots of trendy shops, such as Le Fortune and Le Veintinueve, and El Born is a favourite spot for boutiques. El Raval is catching up fast: Caníbal, at Carrer del Carmé 5, has fun, one-off designs, while Carrer de la Riera Baixa is lined with vintage and second-hand clothes shops.

Shoes

These are great value. Look for Catalan and Spanish designers such as elegant Farrutx and Lottusse (contemporary classics), both found at Tascón (Passeig de Gràcia and El Born), and Camper (trendy, comfortable shoes) at Passeig de Gràcia and Carrer de Mutaner in Eixample. For espadrilles try century-old La Manual Alpargatera at Carrer d'Avinyó 7. The best areas for shoes and bags are Portal de l'Angel, Rambla de Catalunya, Passeig de Gràcia and Diagonal.

FOOD

The best places to buy food are markets or *colmados* (grocer's shops). Look out for juicy marinated olives, sausages (chorizo and *sobrasada*), ham (*jabugo* is the best), cheese (Manchego, Mahon, Idiazabal), nuts, dried fruit, artisan chocolates, *turrón* (a hard or soft nougat-type delicacy), wine, cava and moscatel.

Some of the city's finest historic food stores include Casa Gispert (Carrer dels Sombrerers 23); Colmado Quilez (Rambla de Catalunya 63); chocolatiers Escribà (La Rambla 83); Fargas (Carrer del Pi 16), for excellent *turrón*; and Xocoa (Carrer de Petritxol 11), whose innovative chocolate flavours include 'live peppers' and 'thyme'.

Múrria (Carrer de Roger de Llúria 85) is home to an exquisite range, including own-label cava, in the prettiest of old Modernista interiors, while Planelles Donat (Portal de l'Angel 7) are specialists in turrón and delicious ice cream.

MARKETS

There are covered markets selling fruit, vegetables, meat and fish, in just about every *barrio*. Most open daily except Sunday from early morning until 3pm. Try to avoid Monday though, when the selection is poor because the central wholesale market does not open. The largest market is La Rambla's Boqueria, which opens till 8.30pm. The bargains are to be found in the maze of stalls at the back.

The intimate Harlem Jazz Club

ENTERTAINMENT

Barcelona is one of the liveliest places in Europe. You will never be bored once the sun's gone down in the city that never sleeps, whether your preference be for clubs or bars, traditional or avant-garde music, film, dance or theatre.

Barcelona is hip, vibrant and buzzing, but it's not just about bars and all-night clubbing. This city is a multicultural melting pot, offering a variety of entertainment from traditional Catalan theatre to avant-garde dance and independent cinema. You can hang out with the cool crowd on the waterfront, listen to a top-class orchestra, or seek out traditional flamenco in an Old Town bar. Live music is an essential part of Barcelona life.There is strong government support for the arts, in particular for film and for those promoting Catalan identity and language.

THEATRE

Avinguda Paral.lel in Poble Sec has long been associated with theatrical and musical productions. This main artery is being revived, and will provide an entertainment and gastronomic hub between Plaça d'Espanya and the port. The theatres, Apolo, Condal and Victoria, are on the route and the old music halls Artèria Paral.lel and El Molino have been restored. It is hoped that the Teatre Arnau will become a cultural centre.

Performances are often in Catalan but many theatres also host music and dance, which may have more appeal to non-Catalan speaking visitors.

Mainstream

Among the most popular theatres, showing a varied programme, is the Teatre Lliure (see page 120); subtitles in English are provided for some shows. The Teatre Poliorama (La Rambla 115) stages comedy, musicals and theatre for children. Other venues such as the L'Antic Teatre (see page 120) and Teatre Guasch (Carrer de Aragó 140) have programmes for all ages and tastes.

Catalan and fringe

The most prominent of the theatres dedicated to the Catalan language is the government-funded Teatre Nacional de Catalunya (see page 120), which also promotes dance. Fringe theatres include the inspiring Sala Beckett (see page 120) and avant-garde La Fura dels Baus (Carrer de Pujades 77–9). The open-air Teatre Grec in Montjuïc (see page 76) makes for an unusual summer experience.

Gran Teatre del Liceu   *Flamenco at Los Tarantos*

MUSIC

Classical and opera

In addition to the permanent venues, you will find performances in churches, museums and palaces. L'Auditori (see page 62) is home to the city's resident orchestra and hosts international and national names. Catalan and top international performers can be found in the glorious setting of the Palau de la Música Catalana (see page 46). For opera fans the stunning Gran Teatre del Liceu (see page 33) is a must; internationally acclaimed singer, Montserrat Caballé was born in Barcelona and studied in the city.

Jazz, rock and pop

There is a strong tradition of jazz, and the Barcelona Jazz Festival (Oct–Dec), has taken place for over 40 years. Among the best places to hear jazz are the legendary Jamboree (see page 120) and the smaller, more intimate, Harlem Jazz Club (see page 120).

The number of venues for music gigs is huge and you can catch some of the famous names from the world of rock and pop at big stadiums such as Camp Nou, Estadi Olímpic and the nearby Palau Sant Jordi arena. But there is also good local talent at smaller venues – try Razzmatazz (see page 121) for all genres of music. If you are here in early summer look out for the popular Sonar and Primavera music festivals.

DANCE

Barcelona's dance scene encompasses everything from ballet, tango and flamenco to a lively contemporary programme. Ballet and other dance forms can be seen at Teatre Lliure, Teatre Nacional and Gran Teatre del Liceu. For contemporary dance don't miss the innovative productions at the Teatre Mercat de les Flors (see page 121). If you want to sample traditional flamenco try Los Tarantos (see page 121); or for a full-blown show go to the more touristy El Tablao de Carmen at the Poble Espanyol in Montjuïc (see page 77).

NIGHTLIFE

On a first visit to Barcelona most people head down the busy La Rambla or mingle around Plaça Reial in the Barri Gòtic for the eclectic mix of bars, clubs and restaurants. Other districts offer distinct nightlife choices: El Born is the place to see and be seen in its chic cocktails bars, while the popular El Raval is the most cosmopolitan and bohemian. The waterfront is a great place to be at night, too – a terrace at Port Vell, a bar in Barceloneta or at Port Olímpic with its discos, bars and casino. For an alternative music scene try the up-and-coming Poble Nou district or head to Eixample, where students, locals and older night owls rub shoulders. In the streets just to the west of here Gaixample can be found, a magnet for gay and lesbian clubbers. See also page 120.

Gaudí's Casa Batlló

MODERNISME

Architecture is on the agenda of many visitors to Barcelona, due mainly to the outlandish works of Antoni Gaudí and his Modernista contemporaries. The city's defining architectural style looked to the past for its main influences.

Modernisme is Barcelona's great contribution to architecture. Colourful and flamboyant, the architectural and artistic style emerged around the time of the Universal Exhibition, held in the Parc de la Ciutadella (see page 60), in 1888 and continued until c.1930, thus corresponding to the Arts and Crafts and Art Nouveau (or Jugendstil, as it was known in Germany and Austria) movements in the rest of Europe. It shared with Arts and Crafts a focus on traditional styles and craftsmanship and, with Art Nouveau, a preoccupation with sinuous lines, organic form and ornament and a rebellion against rigid designs and colourless stone and plaster.

Catalan Renaissance

In Barcelona the new style assumed nationalist motifs and significance, which may be why it has been so carefully preserved. The movement was a part of the Catalan *Renaixença* (Renaissance), which looked to the past, taking on Catalan Gothic and its tradition of iron work, as well as acknowledging the highly elaborate styles of Islamic Spain.

The city's 19th-century expansion (the Eixample) gave architects the freedom and space to experiment, and this area is where the majority of the city's Modernista buildings are located (see page 68).

KEY FIGURES

The movement's greatest practitioners were Antoni Gaudí i Cornet (1852–1926), Lluís Domènech i Montaner (1850–1923), a professor of Barcelona University's School of Architecture, and one of his pupils, Josep Puig i Cadafalch (1867–1957). At the Universal Exhibition Domènech designed what is now the Laboratori de Natura (the former Museu Zoologia, see page 61), based on Valencia's red-brick Gothic Stock Exchange, which afterwards became a workshop for ceramics, wrought iron and glass-making. Furnishings and details were an essential ingredient in Modernista buildings, in the same way that a coherent design was key to Arts and Crafts and Art Nouveau design. In the years immediately following its heyday, Modernisme was considered the epitome of bad taste, but the pendulum has swung back again, and Modernista buildings have become symbols of a vibrant city.

Passeig de Gràcia detail

Park Güell, a Modernista gem

HIGHLIGHTS

Illa de la Discòrdia

The best starting point to understand Modernisme is the 'block of discord', three neighbouring buildings in Passeig de Gràcia. The block gained its name because of the close juxtaposition of three outstanding buildings – Domènech's Casa Lleó Morera, Puig's Casa Amatller and Gaudí's Casa Batlló (see page 69) – each of which is in a conflicting style, although they are all categorised as Modernista.

Gaudí buildings

Having worked under Josep Fontseré on the Parc de la Ciutadella and the Plaça del Rei (see page 40), Gaudí earned his first commission, the Casa Vicens (see page 85) in Gràcia, aged 32. In 1878 he met wealthy textile manufacturer Count Eusebi Güell, whose fortune and passion for experimental architecture – and his ability to accept the architect's wildly imaginative ideas – were crucial to Gaudí's rising star. It led to the building, from 1886–8, of the Palau Güell (see page 55) and, later, from 1900, the Park Güell (see page 73).

Gaudí's other key buildings include La Pedrera (see page 70), on which he worked from 1905, Casa Batlló (see above) and the monumental Sagrada Família (see page 72), on which he worked from 1883; the deeply religious architect was still designing the church,

with its extravagant organic lines, when he died aged 74 in 1926. Catalonia's patron saint was a favourite Modernista theme. Gaudí's Casa Batlló is dedicated to the saint, with spiny dragons' 'bones' for window frames.

Other key works

Other key Modernista works include the Unesco-protected Palau de la Música Catalana (see page 46), an extraordinarily sumptuous building, with a spectacular interior. Its facade, crowded with sculptures and dazzling mosaics, is rather cramped down Carrer de Sant Francesc de Paula. There are daily tours of the building, but it is best to attend a concert beneath the stained-glass dome that suffuses the auditorium with a mellow light.

Hospital de la Santa Creu i Sant Pau (see page 73), designed by Domènech, was the most advanced in Europe when it was completed in 1901. It is essentially a series of pavilions connected by underground tunnels and is one of the Modernista highlights of the city. Also by Domènech, at Carrer de Mallorca 291, is Casa Thomas, built for the engraving business of a relative. The top three storeys and the protruding gallery on the top storey were added by his son-in-law, Francesc Guàrdia.

Key works by Puig i Cadafalch include the Casaramona textile factory, at the foot of Montjuïc, which is now the vibrant CaixaForum cultural centre (see page 77).

Fishmonger sign

CATALAN

Visitors will quickly become aware that Catalan is the official language of Barcelona and Catalonia. Not only are all signs in Catalan, but Catalan is spoken among Barcelonans, even when in a group of non–Catalan speakers.

Catalan is spoken by at least 11.5 million people in Catalonia, Valencia, the Roussillon region of France, Andorra and some border areas of Aragón. It is also spoken in the Balearic Islands and the city of Alghero in Sardinia, both of which were ruled by Catalonia in the 13th to 14th centuries. Catalan is a Romance language, meaning it is Latin based, a sister to Castilian (Spanish), French, Italian and Portuguese. It has a staccato quality that makes it sound very different from Castilian, though when written its similarities are more apparent.

EARLY USE

Catalan began to be used widely from the 13th century, particularly in legal codes, such as the *Consolat de Mar*, which laid down laws governing Mediterranean shipping. The four Great Chronicles describing the life of Jaume I (the Conqueror) are also from this time. One of the families who ended up in Mallorca as a result of Jaume's conquests was that of Ramón Lull (1232–1315), whose religious and philosophic writings in Catalan (as well as Latin and Arabic) were prodigious.

GOLDEN AGE

The Golden Age of Catalan literature was in the 15th century, when Jocs Florals (Floral Games) were introduced as linguistic competitions for troubadors. This was in imitation of similar events in Toulouse in France, where Languedocian, a regional language similar to Catalan, was spoken. *Tirant lo Blanc*, a novel of chivalry written by Joanot Martorell and published in 1490, preceded Miguel de Cervantes' *Don Quixote* by over a century. Viewed by some as the greatest European novel of its century ('the best book of its kind in the world', says the priest in *Don Quixote*), *Tirant* has been translated worldwide.

18TH CENTURY

After the War of Succession (1705–15), Catalonia was punished for siding with the Habsburg Archduke Charles. Castilian became the official language, and Catalan was relegated to religious and popular use. It was not until the industrial revolution, and the emergence of a dynamic middle class

Catalan independence rally   *Bilingual street sign*

during the 19th century, that an economic and cultural revival known as the *Renaixença* (Renaissance) enabled Catalan to recover as a vehicle of culture.

Its leading lights were poets, notably Jacint Verdaguer (1845–1902), a priest, who won many prizes in the Jocs Florals. His poetry is still required reading in schools, and his hymn *El Virolai* is sung daily by the choir at Montserrat monastery. The Catalan nationalist sentiment informed all the arts; Modernisme architecture, which harked back to the Golden Age, can be said to be a showpiece of Catalan aspiration.

20TH CENTURY

In 1907 the Institut d'Estudis Catalans was formed for 'the re-establishment and organisation of all things relating to Catalan culture'. When the Generalitat was set up in 1931, Catalan again enjoyed the status of official language.

However, Franco's victory in the Spanish Civil War (1936–9) stamped out Catalan. It was banned entirely from public use, as were Galician and Basque, the other regional languages of Spain. Books, newspapers and films were subjected to draconian censorship. The enforced implementation of an all-Castilian education system meant that a generation of Catalan speakers were unable to read or write their mother tongue, which they continued to use.

OFFICIAL LANGUAGE

With the recovery of democracy in Spain, Catalan was established alongside Castilian as the official language of Catalonia. Campaigns were launched, and staunch nationalists made their views felt. It was not an easy time: many people in the city are not native Catalans and were worried that their children would be taught in a language they did not understand. But the government set about implementing a policy of 'linguistic normalisation', whereby Catalan was reinstated in all aspects of public life, government and the media. In 1990 the European Parliament passed a resolution recognising Catalan and its use in the European Union.

Nowadays, Catalan thrives in the arts and sciences, the media and advertising. Barcelona is a bilingual city, but there are varying degrees of proficiency. Some older people, educated before the Civil War, may have an imperfect knowledge of Castilian, and, while Catalan is almost universally understood, older immigrants from elsewhere in Spain may not speak it. People schooled during the past two decades are usually proficient in both.

Foreign films shown in the city are increasingly being dubbed into Catalan. The surge in nationalism was highlighted when the centre-right Nationalist Party (CiU) won overall control in Barcelona and Girona in municipal elections in 2011 and Xavier Trias became mayor, the first Catalan nationalist to hold the post.

Depiction of 13th-century Assault on the City of Mallorca

HISTORY: KEY DATES

The city rose to power under Catalonia's medieval count-kings, then fell into decline and subject to the control of Madrid. The urge to break out of this inertia, and a deep Catalan identity, are key to Barcelona's inventive energy.

EARLY HISTORY TO THE GOLDEN AGE

237 BC	The Carthaginian Hamilcar Barca makes a base at Barcino.
206 BC	The Romans defeat the Carthaginians.
AD 531–54	Barcelona is made capital of the Visigoths.
711	Moorish invasion of Spain; they remain until 1492.
878	Wilfred (Guifré) the Hairy founds dynasty of counts of Barcelona.
1096–1131	Ramón Berenguer III extends the Catalan empire.
1213–76	Jaume I consolidates the empire, and expands Barcelona.
1359	The Corts Catalanes (Parliament of Catalonia) is established. The 14th century is the Golden Age of Catalonia.
1395	The Jocs Florals – annual competitions for poets and troubadors – are initiated in Catalonia.

IMPERIAL SPAIN

1469	Ferdinand and Isabella unite Aragón and Castile.
1494	The administration of Catalonia is put under Castilian control.
1516	Carlos I (Charles V, Holy Roman Emperor) takes the throne.
1659	Catalan territories north of the Pyrenees are ceded to France.
1701–13	War of Spanish Succession.
1713–14	Siege of Barcelona by Felipe V's forces; Ciutadella fortress built.
1835	Convents are disbanded by government decree; many are pulled down to give way to such new buildings as the Liceu and Boqueria.
1860	The building of the Eixample, designed by Ildefons Cerdà, begins.
1883	Antoni Gaudí begins work on the Sagrada Família.

THE MODERN ERA

1888	Barcelona hosts its first Universal Exhibition.

The 1929 Universal Exhibition

1897	The café Els Quatre Gats opens and becomes a haunt of artists and writers. Picasso, aged 19, exhibits here for the first time.
1914	The Mancomunitat (provincial government) is formed in Catalonia.
1923	General Primo de Rivera sets up a dictatorship and bans Catalan.
1929	A second Universal Exhibition is held, in the grounds of Montjuïc. Buildings including the Poble Espanyol are constructed.
1931	The Republican party comes to power.
1932	Catalonia is granted a short-lived statute of independence.
1936–9	Civil War ends in Franco's rule and isolates Spain. The Catalan language and the expression of Catalan customs are banned.
1975	Franco dies, and Juan Carlos is made king. Catalan is recognised as an official language.
1979	Statute of Autonomy; Catalan is restored as an official language.
1980	Jordi Pujol becomes president of Catalonia.
1986	Spain joins European Community (European Union). A wave of building begins in preparation for the Olympics.
1992	The Olympic Games are held in Barcelona. 500th anniversary of Columbus's discovery of America and the expulsion of the Moors from Spain.
1994	The Liceu opera house is devastated by fire.

21ST CENTURY

2003	Pujol is replaced as president of Catalonia by Pasqual Maragall.
2004	The city extends north, around Diagonal Mar, for Forum 2004.
2006	A new Catalan statute is passed. Jordi Hereu becomes the third socialist mayor of the city. Maragall stands down, and is replaced by José Montilla as president.
2010	The Sagrada Família is consecrated by Pope Benedict XVI.
2011	Xavier Trias of the Catalan Nationalist party (CiU) is elected mayor in July, ending 32 years of socialist leadership.
2012	Transport work slows with metro link to the airport re-scheduled for 2014. Generalitat President Artur Mas leads a fervent campaign for Catalan independence, aiming for a referendum in 2014.
2013	In the first quarter of 2013 unemployment figures in Spain reach an all-time high of over 6 million (27 percent of the working population). With 57 percent of young people unemployed, many are seeking work abroad.

BEST ROUTES

LA RAMBLA

One of the world's most attractive avenues, La Rambla is the first place any visitor to Barcelona should head for. Animated day and night, it always has something worth seeing – even if it is just the passers-by.

DISTANCE: 1.5km (1 mile)
TIME: 1.5 hours
START: Plaça de Catalunya
END: Port Vell
POINTS TO NOTE: This is an easy stroll that can be done at any time of day. Unfortunately, you need to be on your guard against pickpockets on this popular stretch.

This leafy pedestrian avenue was once a river running beside the old city wall to the sea. On the left as you head down to the port is the Ciutat Vella, the Old Town, with tempting lanes and alleys (see page 36 and see page 42), while signs to the modern Museu d'Art Contemporani (MACBA) and Palau Güell, the only Gaudí building in this area, beckon on the right (southwest), in the old working-class Raval district (see page 52). Traffic rumbles over the cobbles either side of the wide, plane-tree shaded promenade, and you will cross back and forth, as sights and attractions entice.

La Rambla at dusk

PLAÇA DE CATALUNYA

At the top of La Rambla is the **Plaça de Catalunya ❶**, where the Old Town ends and the new city (the Eixample, see page 68), laid out during the early 20th century and extending inland, begins. A pavement star in the middle of this large open square marks the geographical heart of the city. Plaça de Catalunya is the city's main transport hub, with a warren of underground passages leading to both FGC trains (for the suburbs) and national Renfe trains; several metro lines also stop here.

The 1925 **El Corte Inglés** (The English Style) department store is on the northeast side of the square. The airport bus stops beside it, and nearby is the 'i' sign of the underground **tourist information centre**. An angular monument by local sculptor Josep María Subirachs commemorates Francesc Macià (1859–1933), president of the Generalitat before the Civil War. Chess players tend to gather nearby. Flanking the square to the southwest is the popular **Café Zurich,** see ❶.

LA RAMBLA

From here the **Rambla** (from the verb *ramblar*, meaning to stroll) begins, a 1.2km (1-mile) promenade of colourful stalls selling such items as birds, flowers, newspapers and magazines, with pavement cafés sheltered beneath its established plane trees. Musicians, mime artists, tango dancers, fire eaters, fortune tellers and other entertainers add to the diversion day and night.

A fashionable place to stroll since the 19th century, La Rambla is in fact made up of five different *rambles*: Canaletes, Estudis, Sant Josep, Caputxins and Santa Mònica, the last three taking their names from convents that lined the southwest (right-hand) side of the street, giving it the name of 'Convent Way'. In the 1830s these powerful institutions were reduced by riots and reforms. Until the 15th century, the city wall ran down the southwestern side of the avenue.

Top of the avenue

The first section, **Rambla de Canaletes**, takes its name from the 19th-century **Font de Canaletes ❷** drinking fountain, now a popular meeting place. Jubilant Barça fans traditionally gather here to celebrate their team's victories. The story goes that if you drink from the fountain's waters, you are sure to return to Barcelona. If, however, you would prefer a taste of something less puritanical, make a brief detour left into Carrer dels Tallers, for **Boadas**, see ❷.

Back on the main street, the next stretch is the **Rambla dels Estudis**, named after the university that was here until 1714. At No. 115, on the right, is **Poliorama ❸** (www.teatrepoliorama.com), a 64-seat theatre, where comedies and musicals are the mainstay. Its upper floors house the Royal Academy of Sciences and Arts. Look up to see the

Miró's pavement by Pla de la Boqueria

city's first clock, erected in 1888 and inscribed *Hora Oficial* (Official Time).

Palau Moja

Opposite, beyond the Hotel Rivoli, is the colonnade of the bookshop of the Generalitat (Catalonia's autonomous government), which has maps and lavish books on the city and region. The shop occupies part of the ground floor of the 18th-century, neoclassical **Palau Moja** ❹ (Carrer de la Portaferrissa 1; tel: 93 316 27 40; call ahead to arrange a visit; free), belonging to the Generalitat's Department of Culture. It hosts temporary exhibitions and is worth dipping into to see the fine first-floor Grand Salon's Baroque murals by Francesc Pla (1743–92). The main entrance to the palace, and to the courtyard, is in Carrer de la Portaferrissa, once one of the main alleys into the Old Town. Today the lively shopping street is popular for shoes, fashion and leather goods.

Mare de Déu de Betlem

Opposite the palace across La Rambla is the **Mare de Déu de Betlem** ❺ (Carrer del Carme 2; free), a 17th-century Baroque church, bare since being burnt out in the Civil War and only recently renovated. This was part of a Jesuit convent, and a statue of the order's founder, the Basque-born saint, Ignatius Loyola, is joined by St Boromeu to flank the entrance. Since 1963 the church has staged charming displays of carefully crafted nativity scenes

(pessebres), from mid-November until February.

Palau de la Virreina

Beyond the church, the pavement is set back to give a grand vista of the **Palau de la Virreina** ❻ (La Rambla 99; www.virreina.bcn.cat; Tue–Sun noon–8pm; free), an imposing rococo building with lavish masonry and metalwork decoration. It was completed in 1777 for Manuel Amat, Spain's pleasure-loving viceroy to Peru, but he died shortly after taking up residence. His widow lived here for many years hence the name: 'Palace of the Viceroy's Wife'.

Built around two courtyards, it is now called the Virreina Centre de la Imatge, and partially open as a centre for cultural events and major exhibitions. At the front of the building is a box office for events in the city.

Beside the palace is the dinky Modernista **Casa Beethoven**, which has been selling sheet music since 1920. On the other side of the street, at No. 96, the first-floor **Museu de l'Eròtica** (www.erotica-museum.com; daily June–Sept 10am–midnight, Oct–May 10am–10pm; charge) showcases saucy artworks, photographs and sculptures, etc.

La Boqueria

The 19th-century Mercat de Sant Josep, better known as **La Boqueria** ❼ (www.boqueria.info; Mon–Sat 8am–8.30pm), is named after the convent that stood just past the Palau de la

Fresh fruit at La Boqueria   *Jamón, jamón at La Boqueria*

Virreina. Here, top restaurateurs and other gourmets do their early-morning shopping. Look out for fungi in season, super-fresh vegetables and fruit, delectable ranges of olives, cheeses and nuts, butchers' stalls selling all you need for nose-to-tail eating, plus seafood glistening on ice.

Just beyond the market on the corner of Carrer Petxina is an attractive mosaic-fronted Modernista shop, the **Antigua Casa Figueras**. It now houses the **Pastilería Escribà**, see ❸, owned by the Barcelona chocolate-producing dynasty, the Escribà family.

Pla de la Boqueria

In front of the market is the square of the same name, **Pla de la Boqueria** ❽. At the point where it breaks up the line of trees, lanes on the left lead into the Barri Gòtic (see page 42). Pla de la Boqueria was once the place of public executions. Nowadays, it is a considerably more pleasant place, enlivened by a colourful mosaic pavement by Joan Miró.

Beside it is **Casa Bruno Quadras**, built in the Oriental style, decorated with fans, lanterns and an elaborate coiling green Chinese dragon by Josep Vilaseca. It was originally designed to house an umbrella shop in the mid-1880s, but now shelters a savings bank.

Gran Teatre del Liceu

The block from Carrer de Sant Pau to Carrer de la Unió is taken up by the **Gran Teatre del Liceu** ❾ (www.liceubarcelona.cat; tours daily 10am; charge). The limited facilities inside this classic, plush 19th-century opera house were improved when the building was reconstructed following a major fire in 1994. One of the city's great institutions, it attracts world-renowned opera stars and also hosts jazz, cabaret and film (including some free entertainment in the foyer). There is a shop and café in the basement, though the historic **Cafè de l'Opera**, see ❹, opened in 1929 and one of the few remaining traditional cafés in the city, is just on the other side of La Rambla.

Boqueria breakfast

The market is a great place to eat at any time of the day, but for a special experience come early for an *esmorçar de cullera*, a hearty breakfast. The 18-seater El Quim de la Boqueria (www.elquimdelaboqueria.com) is where local foodies gather from 7am for breakfast prepared by Quim Márquez, whose innovative dishes include *fricassée* of artichokes and white asparagus, fried egg with sautéed mushrooms topped with caramel foie, and tiny clams steamed in sparkling wine. Pinotxo, open from 6am, is a lively market tapas bar specialising in Catalan cuisine, and there is always a warm welcome here from the Bayen family. Alternatively, try the equally busy Kiosk Universal (see page 111).

Oriental dragon on Casa Bruno Quadras

Vintage hotels

Many historic hotels line La Rambla, among them the **Oriente** (see page 101), just beyond the Liceu. The interior cloister of the Franciscan college on which it was built, remains intact.

The first turning on the right after the Oriente is **Carrer Nou de la Rambla**, housing, just along on the left, at Nos 3–5, **Palau Güell** (see page 55), the only building by Gaudí in the Old Town.

Plaça Reial

Opposite Carrer Nou de la Rambla, a faded grand arch leads into the **Plaça Reial** ❿, one of the city's liveliest squares. Beneath its colonnades are cafés and tapas restaurants. At No. 17 is legendary jazz club, **Jamboree** (www.masimas.com; daily 8pm–11am; charge), which has been here since the 1960s. Top jazz musicians perform in its intimate vaulted basement and it also hosts club nights and Latin, funk, soul and hip-hop acts.

Towards the port

After the Plaça Reial, the Rambla opens up on the left into **Plaça del Teatre** ⓫, where portrait artists ply their trade and old men sit for hours over coffee in a traditional café. Barcelona's first theatre was on this site, and Frederic Soler (1835–95), founder of its present incarnation, the **Teatre Principal**, is commemorated in an imposing statue. He is unfortunately best known these days because a public toilet has been built beneath the statue – a great relief (literally), as bars are increasingly unwelcoming to non-clients using their facilities.

Further down, at La Rambla 7, on the right, is the **Centre d'Art Santa Mònica** ⓬ (www.artssantamonica.cat; Tue–Fri 11am–9pm, Sat 3–8pm; free). The former cloisters have been converted into three storeys of open gallery space. The second-floor bar and café offer views

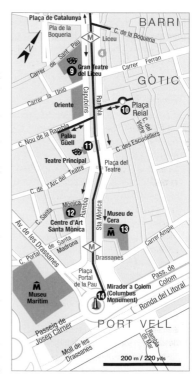

Carrer del Colom arcades   *Lively Plaça Reial*

over the Rambla. A cultural information centre is on the ground floor.

The old-fashioned green ticket booth in the middle of La Rambla sells tickets for the **Museu de Cera** ⓑ (Wax Museum; Passatge de la Banca; www.museocerabcn.com; summer daily 10am–10pm, winter Mon–Fri 10am–1.30pm, 4–7.30pm, Sat–Sun 11am–2pm, 4.30–8.30pm; charge). More than 360 waxworks of mainly Spanish personalities appear in this handsome former bank. Also inside is the café El Bosc de les Fades, an enchanted 'forest' with magically lit gnarled trees and gnomes.

Mirador a Colom

You can't miss the 50m (165-ft) high **Mirador a Colom** ⓮ (Columbus Monument; tel: 93 302 52 24; daily 10am–8.30pm; charge), designed by Gaietà Buigas, with a crowning sculpture of Columbus by Rafael Arché. Columbus is not pointing towards the New World, as intended; locals claim that he is simply pointing to the sea. For a great view, take the elevator to the top.

Just south of the statue is the seafront and **Port Vell**, where the Rambla turns into the **Rambla de Mar** (see page 56), a walkway over to the marina.

Food and Drink

❶ CAFÉ ZURICH

Plaça de Catalunya; tel: 93 317 91 53; daily 8am–11pm; €

This city institution was rebuilt as part of El Triangle commercial centre for the 1992 Olympics. Slow down at its pavement tables, which spill onto the square, and choose from café standards of sandwiches, salads, etc., plus delicious pastries and coffee.

❷ BOADAS

Carrer dels Tallers 1; tel: 93 318 95 92; www.boadascocktails.com; Mon–Sat noon–2am; €

Barcelona's oldest cocktail bar, with 1930s decor and caricatures of the original owner. He mixed a mean *mojito*, a skill learned from his Cuban parents; his daughter, Dolores, continues the tradition.

❸ PASTILERIA ESCRIBÀ

Rambla de les Flores 83; tel: 93 301 60 27; www.escriba.es; Mon–Thu noon–5pm, 8–11pm, Sat–Sun noon–5pm; €

Just one outlet of the famous Escribà patisserie and chocolate makers, with fare as enchanting as its facade.

❹ CAFÈ DE L'OPERA

La Rambla 74; tel: 93 317 75 85; www.cafe operabcn.com; daily 8.30am–2.30am; €€

Open all day long, this historic café with old-time waiters, consummate professionals in traditional attire, is an ideal choice for a break at any time of day. It does good breakfasts, and is a favourite pit stop among the opera crowd after a performance.

The area's atmospheric alleyways

ROYAL BARRI GÒTIC

The complex comprising the cathedral and royal palace is at the heart of the Old Town, which also incorporates a chunk of Roman Barcino. These imposing constructions contrast with the area's delicate cloisters and narrow lanes.

DISTANCE: 1.5km (1 mile)
TIME: 3–4 hours
START: Avinguda del Portal de l'Angel
END: Plaça del Rei
POINTS TO NOTE: This is an easy stroll through the pedestrianised streets of one of the most complete medieval quarters in Europe. Note that these lanes tend to be very busy on Saturdays.

This walk starts at the bottom of Plaça de Catalunya, once the location of the Portal de l'Angel, the main inland gate into the medieval city. It can be combined with elements of the following walk, covering the 'Official Barri Gòtic', (see page 42).

AVINGUDA DEL PORTAL DE L'ANGEL

The busy **Avinguda del Portal de l'Angel ❶** leads into the Barri Gòtic from the Plaça de Catalunya. This wide shopping thoroughfare is ideal if you are hunting for shoes or moderately priced fashion.

Santa Anna

Iron gates halfway down the first turning on the right, **Carrer de Santa Anna**, lead to the two-tiered Gothic cloisters of the medieval church of **Santa Anna ❷** (Mon–Sat 11am–7pm, Aug closes 2pm; free). Built for the Knights Templar in the 12th century, the church's cloister and chapter house are still intact.

The Necropolis

From Santa Anna go down Carrer de Bertrellans, opposite the wonderful fan shop Guantería Alonso, into **Plaça de la Vila de Madrid ❸**, which has been modelled to show off a Roman necropolis, discovered in the 1950s. However, it is rather overpowered by the large Decathlon sports store, which dominates the square.

Opposite, at Carrer de la Canuda 6, is a palatial 18th-century mansion that houses the **Ateneu Barcelonès** cultural centre. Inside are fine paintings by Francesc Pla. It holds temporary exhibitions, a good restaurant (see page 111) and an attractive garden.

Catedral de Santa Eulàlia

Museu d'Història de la Ciutat

Els Quatre Gats

Return to Avinguda del Portal de l'Angel and just back up the street on the far side is Carrer de Montsió, where tucked away is Casa Martí, a fine Modernista building designed in 1897 by architect Puig i Cadafalch. It is famous as **Els Quatre Gats** ❹ (The Four Cats), see ❶, an arty café frequented by Barcelona's artists around the start of the 20th century.

Art colleges

Continue down Avinguda del Portal de l'Angel, and as you take a left fork into Carrer dels Arcs, you will see the restored Modernista Hotel Catalonia Catedral at No. 10. Continue to the **Institute Barcelonès d'Art**, home of the Reial Cercle Artístic, which has a restaurant (see page 112) and exhibition space.

Beyond it on the left is the **Col.legi d'Arquitectes**, the facade surmounted by a frieze designed by Picasso and executed by the Norwegian artist Carl Nesjar. Reminiscent of cave drawings and completed in 1961, it was Picasso's first work to appear in Spain since his self-imposed exile after the Civil War.

ROMAN GATES

The lane now opens out on to **Avinguda de la Catedral** ❺. The Roman wall that encircled the 4th-century city begins its surviving 1.5km (1-mile) stretch here. The wall, constructed using colossal stones, the largest of which is some 3.5m (12ft) thick and 9.5m (30ft) high, originally had 78 square towers, of which several remain.

One tower forms the **Portal del Bisbe** ❻, beside which you can see remains of the aqueduct that brought water to the Roman city. Through this 'gate' on the right is the

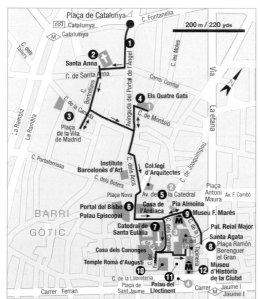

The famously bad-tempered cathedral geese

Palau Episcopal (Bishops' Palace; tel: 93 270 10 12), built in 1769 around the 12th-century courtyard, which is visible through the main entrance.

The interiors of three other Roman towers can be seen in the **Casa de l'Ardiaca** (Archdeacon's House; tel: 93 318 11 95; free), next to the cathedral. The house has an attractive patio, where a palm tree towers over a fountain. Note the letter box decorated with swallows and tortoises – signifying swift and slow mail – added in 1908 by Modernista architect Domènech i Montaner. Facing the Casa de l'Ardiaca is the atmospheric Romanesque chapel of **Santa Eulàlia**, built in 1269 and one of the earliest parts of the cathedral, which it adjoins.

CATEDRAL DE SANTA EULÀLIA

There has been a Christian church on Plaça de la Seu, the site of the present cathedral, since the 10th century. The first was destroyed by Al-Mansur, vizier of Córdoba, in ad985. The current **Catedral de Santa Eulàlia** ❼ (www. catedralbcn.org; daily 8am–7.30pm; cloister daily 8.30am–7pm; free, charge for some areas and donation requested between 1.30pm and 5pm) was begun in 1298 under Jaume II and completed in 1417, though its main, west facade was not finished until the early 20th century. Long-term restoration means that scaffolding may be in place. For a good view of the Barri Gòtic and a close-up of the spires, take the elevator from the nave (to the left of the entrance) to the roof of the cathedral (charge).

Cathedral interior and cloisters

The austere, lofty cathedral has three naves and a central choir. Below the altar is the crypt of St Eulàlia, whose remains were placed here 1,000 years after she was martyred in the Roman purges of Dacian; her alabaster tomb, behind the altar, was carved in 1327. Of the 29 side chapels, the most notable is that of St Salvador, which features a *Transfiguration* (1442) by Bernat Martorell.

A plaque in the baptistery (left of the entrance), notes that the first six Carib Indians brought to Europe by Columbus were baptised here on 1 April 1493. In the Chapel of Christ Lepanto, (right of the entrance), is the crucifix borne in battle by the Christian flagship in the decisive Battle of Lepanto (1571), which defeated the Ottoman Turks.

Among the cathedral's highlights are its cloisters, which are enclosed by a 15th-century iron railing. The cool ambience is emphasised by the mossy Font de les Oques, a drinking fountain that takes its name from the 13 geese (one for every year that St Eulàlia lived) that reside here. Note on the floor the faint engraving of shoes and scissors reflecting the various guilds (of cobblers and tailors, etc.) that paid for the chapel.

Around the cathedral

Opposite the cathedral is the **Hotel Colón**, see ❷. On the far side of the

The cathedral's lofty interior   *Cathedral façade detail*

square, the Roman wall continues past the 15th-century almshouse, **Pia Almoina**, housing the **Museu Diocesa** (Avinguda de la Catedral 4; www.cultural. arqbcn.cat; Tue−Sat 10am−2pm, 5− 8pm, Sun 11am−2pm; charge), showcasing altarpieces, religious sculpture and other icons.

The wall then runs down Carrer de la Tapineria to **Plaça de Ramón Berenguer el Gran ❽**. The equestrian statue here, of the 12th-century count, who added the French region of Provence to Catalonia by marriage, is by Josep Llimona (1864−1934).

MUSEU FREDERIC MARÈS

To the left of the cathedral, Carrer dels Comtes leads down beside the complex of the former royal palace of the count-kings of Barcelona-Aragón. On the left, at Plaça de Sant Iu 5−6, is the **Museu Frederic Marès ❾** (www.museu mares.bcn.es; Tue−Sat 10am−7pm, Sun 11am−8pm; charge, free first Sun in month). In the 13th century this was the bishop's palace, before becoming home to the counts of Barcelona and the count-kings of Barcelona-Aragón. It now houses an extraordinary collection of mainly religious artefacts brought together by Marès, a wealthy local sculptor who lived in the building and had a studio here until his death, at the age of 97, in 1991. There is a large Romanesque collection, with some particularly fine crucifixes, and even entire portals.

The ground and first floors house the sculpture collection. The Collector's Cabinet takes up the second and third floors, described as 'a museum within a museum'. There are 17 separate halls including the most recent additions, the Weapons Hall and the Gentlemen's Quarter Hall. Memorabilia include toys, pipes and photographs, plus Marès' libary-studio. Sheltered in the courtyard is a pleasant café, see ❸.

Sunday sardana

Every Sunday morning people gather outside the cathedral to dance Catalonia's traditional *sardana*. When the music starts, friends hold hands to form circles, placing any bags they are carrying in the centre of the ring. Anyone can join in simply by slipping in between two people – though not between a man and the woman on his right. When the circles grow too large, breakaway groups form new ones. The serious looks on the dancers' faces are the result of having to keep count of the short, sedate, steps and the bouncy long ones, so that everyone finishes exactly on cue. The accompanying band or *cobla*, has 11 players, and the leader, seated, plays a *flabiol* (three-holed flute) and taps the rhythm on a *tabal* strapped to his arm. Each tune lasts about 10 minutes and in an *audació*, a normal performance, there will be half a dozen tunes. The origins of the music date from the mid-19th century.

Museu Frederic Marès exhibits

TEMPLE ROMÀ D'AUGUSTI

Follow the cathedral's curving walls around Carrer de la Pietat, beside the 14th- to 16th-century **Casa dels Canonges**, and take the first left, Carrer del Paradis. Step inside the entrance of No. 7 to see four Corinthian columns that were part of the **Temple Romà d'August ⓿** (Temple of Augustus; May–Oct Tue–Sat 10am–7pm, Sun 10am–8pm, Nov–Apr Tue–Sat 10am–5pm; free). Set on the highest point in the oppidum, this was the main religious building in Roman times and is now the city's largest single relic from that period.

PALAU DEL LLOCTINENT

Just beyond the Museu Frederic Marès a handsome doorway leads into the elegant courtyard of the **Palau del Lloctinent ⓫**, which takes its name from the Lloctinent (lord lieutenant), who resided here. Part of the former royal palace, and designed in Renaissance style from 1549–57 by Antoni Carbonell, the building was later embellished in Catalan-Gothic style, typified by horizontal lines and solid, plain walls (rather than lofty spaces, as in classic Gothic) between columns, octagonal towers and flat roofs.

PLAÇA DEL REI ✓

Adjacent is the **Plaça del Rei**, the heart of the old royal city. The main royal buildings around the square are accessed through the excellent **Museu d'Història de la Ciutat ⓬** (City History Museum; Plaça del Rei 1; www.museuhistoria.bcn.es; Tue–Sat 10am–7pm, Sun 10am–8pm; charge includes admission to the former royal palace and chapel).

The museum occupies the 17th-century Casa Clariana-Padellàs, a merchant's house that was brought here, stone by stone, in 1930 after the nearby Via Laietana was driven through the Old Town. In the process of re-erecting the house, Roman remains were discovered beneath the ground, and now a huge area of the foundations of the Roman city has been opened up beneath the square. A lift takes visitors down to this subterranean city, which shows streets of shops and industries, from textile dyeing to wine-making.

These ancient stones also chart the development of the first Christian palace that stood here between the 6th and 8th centuries, prefiguring the palace of the Barcelona count-kings.

Palau Reial Major

Emerging from this Roman twilight, you arrive at the **Palau Reial Major**, the former royal palace, dominated by the **Saló del Tinell**, the great hall and throne room. Its enormous interior stone arches were designed in the 14th century for Pere III (the Ceremonious) by Guillem Carbonell, who

Frederic Marès stonework | *Roman columns, Museu d'Història de la Ciutat*

was also responsible for much of the palace's facade. Columbus is said to have been received here by Ferdinand and Isabella. Today, its role is more humble, staging various concerts and exhibitions.

The **Capella Reial de Santa Agata** (Royal Chapel of St Agatha), constructed for Jaume II (the Just) in 1312, features a rare embellishment in an otherwise rather austere complex. Jaume's coat of arms can be seen behind the retable of the Epiphany, painted by Jaume Huguet in 1464–5, while scenes of St Agatha's martyrdom are depicted in a chapel on the left.

ENDING THE WALK

Return to the front of the Museu d'Història de la Ciutat, where small quirky shops include, at No. 7, the candlemakers **Cereria Subirà**, the oldest shop in the city. Stop for a drink or a chocolate and *xurros* (*churros* – chunks of deep-fried batter coated in sugar) at the quaint **Mesón del Café**, see ❹. Alternatively, pick up a pastry from one of the *pastelerías* in this area: *tartaletas de music* ('music tarts' – sweet mixed-nut tartlets) or *empanadas catalanas* (pies filled with tuna and olives) are specialities.

Food and Drink

❶ ELS QUATRE GATS

Carrer de Montsió 3; tel: 93 302 41 40; www.4gats.com; daily 10am–1am; €€
In this historic arts café and restaurant, 19-year-old Pablo Picasso had his first exhibition in 1900. It is very touristy, but still worth a visit: the food is very acceptable and the sense of place is a big pull.

❷ HOTEL COLÓN

Avinguda de la Catedral 7; tel: 93 301 14 04; www.colonhotelbarcelona.com; daily 1–3.30pm, 8–11pm; €€
This elegant, old-fashioned hotel has a good but expensive restaurant, Catedral, but you can also just sit at one of its pavement

tables and enjoy a drink while watching the world go by.

❸ CAFÈ D'ESTIU

Plaça de Sant Iu 5–6; tel: 93 310 30 14; www.cafedestiu.com; Apr–Sept Tue–Sun 10am–10pm; €
This shaded café in the courtyard outside the Museu Frederic Marès serves decent snacks. The name, meaning 'summer café', in Catalan, reflects the fact that it is open only from April to September.

❹ MESÓN DEL CAFÉ

Carrer de la Llibreteria 16; tel: 93 315 07 54; Mon–Sat 7am–11pm; €
This quaint little café has been going since 1909. Perch on a bar stool for a delicious coffee or thick, rich hot chocolate and *xurros*.

Palau de la Generalitat

OFFICIAL BARRI GÒTIC

This tour of the Gothic quarter centres on the government buildings on the area's main square, Plaça de Sant Jaume, and also takes in the Jewish quarter. In the surrounding streets you will find some of the city's most engaging old shops.

DISTANCE: 2km (1.25 miles)
TIME: 3–4 hours
START: Pla de la Boqueria
END: Carrer de Ferran/La Rambla
POINTS TO NOTE: It is easy to feel disorientated in the narrow streets of this quarter, but rest assured that you will never be far from Plaça de Sant Jaume on this roughly circular walk.

Halfway down La Rambla by the Liceu metro, the dragon on Casa Bruno Quadras on **Pla de la Boqueria ❶** marks the corner of Carrer del Cardenal Casañas. This lane of book- and print-sellers sets the tone for the walk and leads into one of the most characterful parts of the **Barri Gòtic**.

SANTA MARIA DEL PI

Among the highlights of the Barri Gòtic are **Plaça del Pi** and the adjacent **Plaça de Sant Josep Oriol**. Dominating both squares is the 14th-century Catalan-Gothic **Santa Maria del Pi ❷**, dis-

tinguished by its stained glass, much of it replaced after being destroyed in 1936 during the Civil War.

Plaça del Pi's handsome architecture includes the wonderful Modernista facade on La Gavineteria Roca, purveyors of cut-throat razors since 1911.

Carrers de Petritxol and de la Palla

In the northwest corner of Plaça del Pi is **Carrer de Petritxol**, a little street of art galleries and independent shops. Sala Parés, at No.5, dates from 1845 and was the first gallery to exhibit work by Pablo Picasso. **Carrer de la Palla**, off Plaça de Sant Josep Oriol, is lined with antiques stores and bookshops, such as Angel Batlle, at No. 23, which also has a wide selection of old prints.

Carrer de Banys Nous

Halfway up the street, take a right turn down **Carrer de Banys Nous ❸**, a delightful street with further antiques stores and bric-a-brac sellers. At No. 11 you'll find Artesania Catalunya, home to crafts workshops. At the end of the street, on the corner of Carrer del Call, is

The Palau's entrance   *Exquisite facade on Plaça del Pi*

the hat shop Sombrereria Orbach, selling Borsalinos and genuine Catalan berets.

JEWISH QUARTER

The narrow, sunless lanes between Plaça del Pi and Plaça de Sant Jaume are redolent of medieval Barcelona. Here, the pleasure is simply in walking the streets, peering into patios, window shopping, menu reading and wondering at the history heaped up behind walls of solid stone.

Much of this area was the *call*, or **Jewish quarter** – the word comes from the Hebrew *qahqal*, meaning 'meeting' – with a large Jewish population here from the 12th century until 1391. That year, following widescale rioting in the wake of accusations that the Jews had brought the plague to Spain, the *call* was virtually destroyed, many of its residents murdered, and the rest given the choice of conversion or expulsion. A century later all non-Catholic religions were banned altogether.

The synagogue

Turn left into Carrer del Call, then first left and first right into Carrer Marlet. At No. 5 is the restored medieval **Sinagoga Shlomo Ben Adret** ❹ (www.callde barcelona.org; Mon–Fri 11am–5.30pm, Sat–Sun 11am–3pm (summer opens at 10.30am); charge), once the largest synagogue in the city.

Museu del Calçat

Carrer Marlet leads into Carrer de Sant Domènec del Call, where you should turn left and stroll up to the attractive, shady **Plaça de Sant Felip Neri** ❺. At No. 5, once the location of the shoemakers' guild, is the **Museu del Calçat** (Museum of Footwear; Tue–Sun 11am–2pm; charge), which showcases

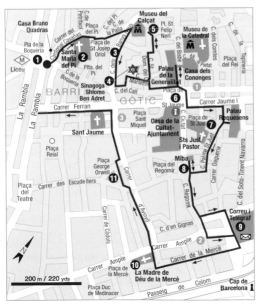

Carrer de Ferran is lined with shops

the history of the craft from Roman times to the present day. Highlights include a huge pair of shoes made to fit the statue of Christopher Columbus at the bottom of the Rambla. They are said to be the largest shoes in the world.

Also overlooking Plaça de Sant Felip Neri is the chic Hotel Neri, housed in a lovely 18th-century mansion.

PLAÇA DE SANT JAUME

Carrer del Call emerges at the **Plaça de Sant Jaume ❻**, the administrative heart of the city, where the Roman Forum once stood. The square is a focal point for celebrations and home to **Conesa**, see ❶, a good place for a snack.

Palau de la Generalitat

The left-hand side of the square is dominated by the imposing Gothic and Renaissance **Palau de la Generalitat** (wwwgencat.net; tours second and fourth Sun of month 10am–1.30pm; free), from where Catalonia is governed. It is topped by a statue of St George, the patron saint of Catalonia, and is decked with red roses (and opened to the public) on his saint's day: 23 April. The 15th-century chapel by Marc Safont and the first-floor **Patí dels Tarongers** (Orange Tree Patio) are among its highlights.

The lane leading up the right-hand side of the Generalitat is the Carrer del Bisbe. On the right is the 14th-century **Casa dels Canonges** (Canons' House),

now Generalitat offices. A neo-Gothic bridge, based on the Venetian Bridge of Sighs, links the two buildings.

Ajuntament

Facing the Generalitat on Plaça de Sant Jaume is the **Ajuntament**, or Casa de la Ciutat, Barcelona's town hall (tours Sun 10am–1.30pm). The entrance is flanked by the figures of Jaume I and Joan Fiveller, a 15th-century councillor who established city freedoms. The building's two most notable rooms are the 14th-century Saló del Consell de Cent and the Saló de les Cròniques, where, in 1928, Josep Maria Sert painted scenes from the 14th-century Catalan expedition to Byzantium. There is a tourist information office on the ground floor.

SOUTH OF SANT JAUME

Go down Carrer de Jaume I, taking the second right into Carrer de Dagueria. This lane leads into **Plaça de Sant Just ❼**, a quiet square overlooked by the church of **Sants Just i Pastor**.

An alley opposite leads down to **Palau Requesens**, home to the Reial Acadèmia de Bones Lletres, built against the **Roman wall**, which runs down Carrer del Sots-Tinent Navarro.

Head down Carrer de la Palma Sant Just and turn right at the bottom onto **Plaça del Regomir ❽**. On the left, note part of the Roman city's southern gate.

Plaça de Sant Miquel

To the right, at Carrer de la Ciutat 4, is **Miba** (Museu d'idees i invents de Barcelona; www.mibamuseum.com; Mon–Fri 10am–2pm, 4–7pm, Sat 10am–8pm, Sun 10am–2pm; charge), a modern museum dedicated to ideas, inventions and creativity.

Continue down Carrer del Regomir, past **El Tropezón**, see ❷, to Carrer d'en Gignas or Carrer Ample, and turn left for the **Correu i Telègraf** ❾ (Post Office). It is worth popping in to admire the decoration by *Noucentiste* artists Canyellas, Galí, Labarta and Obiols.

Outside is *Cap de Barcelona*, a 64m (210ft) cartoon-like portrait of a woman's head by American Pop artist Roy Lichtenstein. Inspired by Gaudí, the work is made from broken tiles.

La Madre de Déu de la Mercè
Walk down Carrer de la Mercè to the church of **La Madre de Déu de la Mercè** ❿ (Plaça de la Mercè; daily 10am–1pm, 6–8pm; free), topped by a statue of the Madonna and child that can be seen from out to sea. La Mercè is the patron saint of Barcelona, and on her saint's day, 24 September, huge models, known as giants, and human pyramids greet the dignitaries coming out from Mass at the start of the festivities.

Carrer d'Avinyó
From the church, head up **Carrer d'Avinyó**, home to two city landmarks: La Manual Alpargatera, at No. 7, which sells espadrilles; and the Modernista **El Gran Cafè**, see ❸. Halfway down on the right is **Plaça George Orwell** ⓫, named after the author of *Homage to Catalonia*.

Turn left at the top of Carrer d'Avinyó, into the shopping street of Carrer de Ferran, which takes you back to La Rambla.

Food and Drink

❶ CONESA
Plaça de Sant Jaume 10; tel: 93 310 13 94; www.conesaentrepans.com; Mon–Sat 8.15am–10.15pm; €
A popular place famous for its delicious, inexpensive hot sandwiches with fillings including tortilla or ham and tomato.

❷ EL TROPEZÓN
Carrer del Regomir 26; tel: 93 310 18 64; Thu–Tue noon–2am; €
Small, authentic tapas bar with a rustic feel and buzzing atmosphere.

❸ EL GRAN CAFÈ
Carrer d'Avinyó 9; tel: 93 318 79 86; www.restaurantelgrancafe.com; Sun–Thu 1pm–midnight, Fri–Sat 1pm–12.30am; €€€
This historic café has a handsome Modernista interior with huge chandeliers. Rather expensive but has a good-value set lunch.

Palau de la Música Catalana

SANT PERE

An enticing marriage of old and new, this eastern corner of the Old Town, northwest of El Born, is where the rag trade once flourished. Its highlights include the Palau de la Música Catalana and the Mercat de Santa Caterina.

DISTANCE: 3km (2 miles)
TIME: 3 hours
START: Palau de la Música
END: Mercat de Santa Caterina
POINTS TO NOTE: This walk is best done in the morning, both to avoid the queues at the Palau de la Música Catalana and to arrive at the market in time for lunch.

In the city's Golden Age, the 14th century, Sant Pere was the residential area favoured by the city's wealthy merchants. As the centre of Barcelona's textile trade, it flourished, but mass-production from the late 19th century led to its demise. Visitors have only recently started exploring its historic streets.

PALAU DE LA MÚSICA

Start at the **Palau de la Música Catalana ❶** (Carrer de St Francesc de Paula 2; www.palaumusica.cat; guided tours daily 10am–3.30pm, Easter and July 19am–6pm, Aug 9am–8pm; booking advisable; charge), built in 1908 by Lluís Domènech

i Montaner and now a World Heritage Site. A Modernista extravaganza, it features lavish decoration of tiles, mosaics and statuary reflecting the Catalan musical tradition. Oscar Tusquets' recent extension, featuring organic motifs in keeping with the Modernista original, houses a concert hall for chamber music and a restaurant. Tours of the building allow you to admire the stained glass and sculptural decoration of the auditorium.

SANT PERE MÉS ALT

Opposite the Palau, at Carrer Sant Pere Més Alt 1, is the **Casal de Gremi de Velers ❷** (Silk Industry Guild), distinguished by fine *esgrafiat* (decorative

---

Food and Drink

❶ BAR MUNDIAL
Plaça de St Augusti Vell 1; tel: 93 319 90 56; Mon–Sat 1–4pm, 8.30pm–midnight; €€
Opened in 1955 and little changed, this local gem does great seafood tapas.

Palau statuary and chandelier

Mercat de Santa Caterina

relief work). This street was the focus of the medieval trade. It ends at Plaça de Sant Pere and the church of **Sant Pere de les Puelles** ❸, a former Benedictine monastery. The street opposite leads to **Plaça de St Augusti Vell** ❹ and its **Bar Mundial**, see ❶.

MERCAT DE SANTA CATERINA

Now take **Carrer dels Carders**, continue to Plaça de la Lana, then right for the **Mercat de Santa Caterina** ❺ (Mon 7.30am–2pm, Tue–Wed, Sat 7.30am–3.30pm, Thu–Fri 7.30am–8.30pm). This stunning three-storey building by the late Enric Miralles is the centre of urban renewal in the area. Its wonderful roof has coloured tiles above and wood below, in arches like upturned boats. Excavations carried out beneath the market have revealed archaeological remains that are partially open to the public.

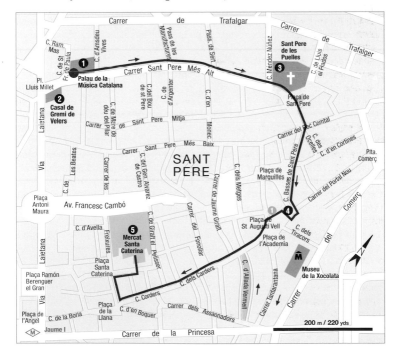

Plaça Santa Maria del Mar tapas bar

LA RIBERA AND EL BORN

The part of the Old Town north of the Via Laietana is La Ribera, a former noble quarter whose name (The Shore) reflects its commercially advantageous waterfront position; within La Ribera is El Born. History mixes with fashion and culture here, with chic boutiques, bars and some of the city's top museums.

DISTANCE: 3km (2 miles)
TIME: 4 hours
START: Jaume I metro
END: Estació de França
POINTS TO NOTE: Start early to avoid queues at Museu Picasso (free on first Sun of month).

This close-knit residential area owes its character to Jaume I (the Conqueror), under whom Catalonia flourished in its Golden Age of the 14th century. The city's rich were businessmen, not aristocrats, and it was in this waterfront area that merchants brought their wares ashore. They traded in the new stock exchange, prayed in Santa Maria del Mar, jousted on the tilting field of El Born and entertained in the sumptuous mansions they erected, notably along Carrer de Montcada.

In later times, a young Pablo Picasso studied at the local art school, where his father also taught; nowadays the Museu Picasso is the area's big crowd-puller.

Many streets in this area are named after *gremis*, the powerful trade guilds, whose duty was to look after the interests of their members. These include Agullers (needle makers), Argenteria (silversmiths) and Sombreres (hatmakers).

CARRER MONTCADA

Start at the **Jaume I metro** ❶ and stroll down Carrer de la Princesa, which divides the Sant Pere district from La Ribera. Opposite **UDON**, Barcelona's first noodle bar, turn right into the slim **Carrer de Montcada**. Named after the fallen in the conquest of Mallorca, it linked the waterfront with the commercial areas during the Golden Age, and the architecturally lavish Catalan-Gothic merchants' mansions that line it reflect its former wealth. Montcada has become museum-street supreme, since the authorities started renovating its medieval palaces in 1957.

There are lots of good pit stops near here, such as **Espai Barroc**, see ❶.

Museu Picasso
At Carrer de Montcada 15–23 is the **Museu Picasso** ❷ (www.museupicasso.

Pintxo tapas in La Ribera   *Museu Picasso*

bcn.es; Tue–Sun 10am–8pm; charge), spread over five imposing mansions. The entrance is at No. 15, the Palau Aguilar, with a handsome courtyard and first-floor gallery by Marc Safont, architect of the inner patio of the Generalitat. This mansion is connected internally to Palau del Baró de Castellet at No. 17, then by Palau Meca Casa Mauri and Palau Finestres, the last two used for temporary exhibitions.

There are over 4,000 artworks in the collection, mainly from Picasso's formative years, with sketches in school books and a masterly portrait of his mother, done when he was just 16. Studies for *Las Meninas* from the 1950s are among the few later works. The museum also has an attractive café. Alongside the existing exhibition halls a new building was opened in 2011 to house a Knowledge and Research Centre.

Museu Europeu d'Art Modern

Opposite the Museu Picasso, a short detour west along Barra de Ferro takes you to the **Museu Europeu d'Art Modern** (MEAM; Barra de Ferro 5; www.meam.es; Tue–Sun 10am–7pm; charge). Opened in 2011, this interesting museum offers

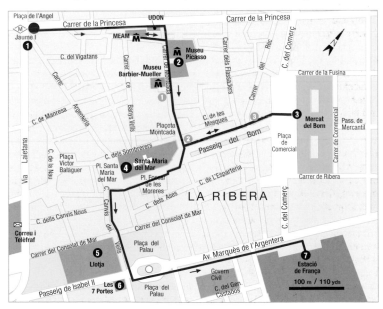

The soaring Santa Maria del Mar

an original and different vision of contemporary art; its objective is to promote figurative art from the late 19th century to the present day. Housed in the stunning 18th-century Palau Gomis, the varied and compelling collection of paintings and sculpture covers three floors and is accessed through a wide courtyard lined with sculptures.

Other Montcada galleries

Back on Carrer de Montcada continue along the street for another contemporary art gallery that usually has notable exhibitions: **Galeria Maeght**, housed in the Palau Cervelló at No. 25 (www.maeght.com, Tue–Fri 11am–2pm, 3–7pm, Sat 11am–2pm), is part of the French Maeght gallery group, which owes its success to the early support in Cannes of Provence-based artists Matisse, Bonnard, Van Dongen and Miró.

EL BORN

Carrer de Montcada ends at Plaçeta de Montcada, where it hits the **Passeig del Born**. The main strip here is a fashionistas' haunt, home to chic bars and cafés, such as **Euskal Etxea Taberna**, see ❷, and **Sandwich & Friends**, see ❸, as well as numerous designer boutiques. The atmosphere in El Born is transformed at night: bars that during the day are hidden behind closed doors or lurk in stygian gloom start to wake up around 9pm, and the merry-go-round of tireless barflies continues until about 4am.

Mercat del Born

A detour east along Passeig del Born takes you past Carrer dels Flassaders, where there are more boutiques and, at the end of the Passseig, Josep Fontserè i Mestre's 19th-century wrought-iron **Mercat del Born** ❸, until 1971, a wholesale food market. The structure, now a cultural centre, (www.bcn.cat/elborncentrecultural), features an exhibition of the events in the Born district in the 1700s and the struggles of the Catalan people. There are also temporary exhibitions, bookshop, café and stages for theatre, music and cinema.

SANTA MARIA DEL MAR

At the western end of Passeig del Born is **Santa Maria del Mar** ❹ (Mon–Sat 9am–1.30pm, 4.30–8pm, Sun 10.30am–1.30pm, 4.30–8pm; free), built from 1329–84 by the maritime enterprises that brought wealth to this part of town. It is a fine example of the Catalan-Gothic style, with horizontal lines, flat terraced roofing, open spaces and octagonal towers. Stand by the main door to appreciate the sense of space and the warm light that enters through the rose window. The striking blue window in the second chapel on the left in the ambulatory commemorates the 1992 Olympic Games.

Surrounding squares

In **Plaça Fossar de les Moreres**, the square beside the church, note the iron

Estació de França The mural at Sandwich & Friends

monument topped by a flame; this commemorates the martyrs of the Bourbon succession in 1714. Beyond it, **Plaça de Santa Maria del Mar** is a buzzy square with appealing cafés and bars. Just to the right is **Carrer de l'Argenteria**, one of the busiest restaurant streets in town, where there are regular queues in the evening, as people wait to get into the popular tapas bars and restaurants.

THE LLOTJA

On the opposite (port) side of the square, turn down Carrer dels Canvis Vells, which leads to the Carrer del Consolat de Mar and the **Llotja ❺** (closed to visitors), the former stock exchange – a handsome 14th-century building with a magnificent Gothic hall.

Picasso's father taught at the Escola de Belles Arts (School of Fine Arts) that occupied the upper part of the build-

ing. The **Reial Academia Catalana de Belles Arts de Sant Jordi** (www.rac ba.org; Mon–Fri 10am–2pm, closed Aug) still occupies part of the building. Its small museum has drawings by the 19th-century Romantic painter Mariano Fortuny.

7 Portes

Across the busy Passeig de Isabel II, in an arcaded 19th-century building, is Barcelona's most famous restaurant, **7 Portes ❻** (see page 114). Peek through the windows to see the handsome panelled interior and imagine Picasso, Lorca and the rest of the artistic crowd enjoying a dish of its speciality black rice or paella.

Further along the road is the grand **Estació de França ❼**, the city's original international train terminus, now restored, and well worth a look in for its handsome iron-and-glass 19th-century structure.

Food and Drink

❶ ESPAI BARROC

Carrer de Montcada 20; tel: 93 310 06 73; www.palaudalmases.com; Tue–Sat 8pm–2am, Sun 6–10pm; €€
A cultural highlight in the Palau Dalmases is this Baroque-style bar. There are live recitals on Thursdays.

❷ EUSKAL ETXEA TABERNA

Plaçeta de Montcada 1–3; tel: 93 310 21

85; restaurant: Mon–Sat 1–4pm, 8pm–midnight; bar: Mon–Fri 10–12.30am, Sat–Sun 10–1am; €€€
Superb Basque tapas bar and restaurant.

❸ SANDWICH & FRIENDS

Passeig del Born, 27; tel: 93 310 07 86; Mon–Thu, Sun 9–12.30am, Fri–Sat 9–1.30am; €
Trendy café dominated by a huge mural. A tremendous variety of sandwiches filled with all sorts of unusual combinations.

Busy street

EL RAVAL

The city's old working-class district still has a slightly raw edge that is reminiscent of a seedy past, but urban redevelopment has laid out new spaces and a fabulous contemporary art museum, the MACBA.

DISTANCE: 2.5km (1.52 miles)
TIME: 2 hours
START: La Rambla (top end)
END: Palau Güell
POINTS TO NOTE: This walk runs parallel to La Rambla, on its southwestern side. It is best to do it during the daytime, but not on Tuesday, when MACBA (the Contemporary Art Museum) is closed.

On the opposite side of La Rambla to the Barri Gòtic is the working-class area of the city that was incorporated into the Old Town with the building of the medieval city walls. El Raval (literally, 'The Slum') stretches from La Rambla to the Ronda de Sant Pau and the Avinguda del Paral.lel. The district of old high-rise tenements was once one of the world's most densely populated, with many immigrants from poorer regions of Spain housed here.

The area towards the waterfront was a haunt of sailors, delinquents and addicts. In the 1920s it was dubbed the *Barri Xinès* (*Barrio Chino* in Spanish),

meaning Chinese quarter, though the Chinese were never in evidence here.

Regeneration area

The area has been undergoing a metamorphosis, thanks to municipal funding. Trendy bars, shops and art galleries now sit side by side with more seedy spots: do not be surprised to see sex workers on street corners in broad daylight. Regeneration has been in progress since the late 1990s, with whole blocks of tenements torn down to open up the area. There is still a large immigrant population here, making it one of the most ethnically diverse parts of Europe. El Raval comes to life at night, with a variety of bars and clubs, such as Rita Blue in Plaça de Sant Augustí or Bar Almirall, which dates from 1860, on Carrer de Joaquín Costa.

MACBA

From the top of La Rambla, take the second right down Carrer del Bonsucces and Carrer d'Elisabets. Like all the streets in this area, it retains many good traditional bars and some quirky new

MACBA exhibition   *Basketball game outside the CCCB*

restaurants, including trendy **Dos Palillos** (see page 115) and, on the parallel street, Carrer Pintor Fortuny, the **Biocenter**, see 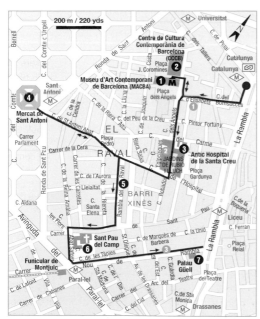 ❶.

Follow signs to Plaça dels Àngels and Richard Meier's ice-white Modernist-style **Museu d'Art Contemporani de Barcelona** ❶ (MACBA; www.macba. cat; June–Sept Mon and Wed–Sat 11am–8pm, Oct–May Mon and Wed–Fri 11am–7.30pm, Sat 10am–8pm, Sun 10am–3pm all year; charge), with the neighbouring Convent dels Àngels acting as an outpost.

The collection

Arranged over three floors, the gallery showcases post-war Catalan, Spanish and international art from c.1950, with works by artists including Antonio Saura, Tàpies, Joseph Beuys, Jeff Wall and Susana Solano. The permanent collection is displayed on a rotating basis, but the main attractions are the cutting-edge temporary exhibitions by contemporary artists. La Central del MACBA is the museum's bookshop and reference centre. **Capella MACBA** is the convent's 15th-century Gothic church with the only Renaissance chapel in Barcelona.

CENTRE DE CULTURA CONTEMPORÀNIA

This melding of ancient and modern, at which the Barcelonans are so good, can be seen again at the Plaça de Joan Coromines, which links the MACBA with the old Casa de Caritat, formerly a poorhouse and orphanage that has become the magnificent, four-storey **Centre de Cultura Contemporània de Barcelona** ❷ (CCCB; Carrer de Montalegre 5; www.cccb.org; Tue–Sun 11am–8pm, exhibition times can vary; charge).

Café on the Rambla del Raval

The centre, which is entered via a ramp in the basement, puts on exhibitions, concerts, dance and films. There is also a bar-restaurant and a bookshop.

Also on Plaça de Joan Coromines is a new university faculty building and the **Centre d'Estudis i Recursos Culturas** (CERC; www.diba.cat/cerc; free). Step inside to see the lovely, tiled 18th-century courtyard, **Pati Manning**, with an Art Deco St George.

At the back of the courtyard is a last vestige of religiosity in the area, the church of **Santa Maria de Montealegre**, where Mass is still held.

ANTIC HOSPITAL DE LA SANTA CREU

Walk back down Carrer dels Àngels to the 15th-century **Antic Hospital de la Santa Creu ❸** (Carrer del Carme/Carrer de l'Hospital; Mon–Fri 9am–8pm, Sat 9am–2pm; free), a convalescent house set up in the 15th century and the city's principal hospital until 1910, when Santa Creu i Sant Paul was built near the Sagrada Família. Some of the building houses the headquarters of the Royal Academy of Medicine, but the rest is devoted to the Massana Art School, the Institute of Catalan Studies and the Library of Catalonia.

On the right as you enter is the Casa de Convalescència (Convalescence House), its gardens richly decorated with 17th-century Baroque tiles by Llo-rens Passolles. Hidden in the gardens is **El Jardi**, a perfect stop for lunch on the terrace, see ❷.

Exit through the main entrance in Carrer de l'Hospital. Just outside is **La Capella** (Tue–Sat noon–2pm, 4–8pm, Sun 11am–2pm; free), the hospital's 15th-century chapel, now an exhibition space for contemporary art.

Carrer de l'Hospital

On **Carrer de l'Hospital** are herbalists, pharmacists and Arab pastry stores, reflecting the quirky mix of traditional and ethnic in this area. One of its side streets, the pedestrian Carrer de la Riera Baixa, is lined with vintage and second-hand clothes shops.

Continuing along Carrer de l'Hospital, head west on to Carrer de Sant Antoni Abat, which extends to **Mercat de Sant Antoni ❹**, a large, attractive 19th-century market hall. During the week this serves as a food market, with clothes and haberdashers' stalls behind the encircling blinds, and on Sunday, from 9am–2pm, it is given over to a lively market for second-hand books, coins and videos. The building is undergoing major restoration, during which the food market has moved to a site close by on the Ronda Sant Antoni. The Sunday book market has been moved just to the north of the main market building. Restoration work is being carried out in phases and there is no definite reopening date as yet.

Sant Pau del Camp   *Palau Güell rooftop view*

Rambla del Raval

Walking back along Carrer de Sant Antoni Abat into Carrer de l'Hospital will bring you to the top of the **Rambla del Raval ❺**. This tree-lined thoroughfare was only relatively recently created by bulldozing more than five blocks through the heart of the *Barri Xinès*, but it has already brought wealth to the area in the shape of bars, galleries and cafes.

SANT PAU DEL CAMP

At the bottom of the Rambla turn right into Carrer de Sant Pau to **Sant Pau del Camp ❻** (Mon 5–8pm, Tue–Sat 10am–1.30pm, 5–8pm, Sat 10am–1.30pm, times may vary; charge), Barcelona's oldest church, dating from Roman times. A door to the right leads to a pretty little cloister with trefoil and cinquefoil arches. A gravestone bears an inscription to Guifre II Borrell, who in 897 became the second ruler of the Barcelona dynasty.

At the crossroads turn left down Carrer de l'Abat Safont.

PALAU GÜELL

Finally, walk down Carrer Nou de la Rambla, past the **London Bar**, see ❸, to the **Palau Güell ❼** (Carrer Nou de la Rambla 3; www.palauguell.cat; Apr–Sept Tue–Sun 10am–8pm, Oct–Mar 10am–5.30pm; charge), designed by Gaudí from 1885–9 as a town house for his patron, Count Eusebi Güell and now reopened after extensive renovation.

With this building, the architect embarked on a period of fertile creativity, alternating elements of the Gothic with Arabic design. The house is structured around an enormous salon, from which a conical roof covered in pieces of tiling emerges to preside over an unusual landscape of capriciously placed battlements, balustrades and strangely shaped chimneys.

Food and Drink

❶ BIOCENTER

Carrer del Pintor Fortuny 25; tel: 93 301 45 83; www.restaurantebiocenter.es; Mon–Sat 1–11pm, Sun 1–4pm; €
This well-established, friendly vegetarian restaurant does healthy, hearty four-course set-price menus.

❷ EL JARDI

Carrer de l'Hospital 56; tel: 93 329 15 50; www.eljardibarcelona.es; Mar–Oct Mon–Sat 10am–11pm, Nov–Feb 10am–10pm; €
In the lovely gardens of the old hospital, this tapas bar is ideal for a freshly produced snack and a drink in the sun or shade.

❸ LONDON BAR

Nou de la Rambla 34; tel: 93 318 52 61; Tue–Sun 7pm–early hours; €
Apart from the addition of a big television screen, this historic pub (established 1910) has changed little since Miró and Picasso drank here. Drinks only, no food.

Port Vell Golondrinas

THE WATERFRONT

Rejuvenated for the Barcelona Olympic Games in 1992, the waterfront area added an exciting new dimension to the city. This tour takes you through Port Vell (Old Port) and the regenerated area of Barceloneta.

> **DISTANCE:** 4km (2.25 miles)
> **TIME:** 3 hours
> **START:** Museu Marítim
> **END:** Torre de Jaume I
> **POINTS TO NOTE:** This is a gentle-paced walk that can be done at any time of day or in the evening.

Commercial maritime activity moved out of Barcelona's original port in the 1990s, leaving Port Vell, the Old Port, with few concerns other than round-the-clock leisure. A focus of the city, this is where people come to spend idle hours, watching vessels from the yacht clubs pass beneath the swing bridge on the pedestrian Rambla de Mar.

On the northeast (or far) side of the port is Barceloneta, the old fishermen's quarter, while on the south side is the cruise-line terminal.

OLD SHIPYARDS

Beyond the bottom of La Rambla are the Drassanes, the city's formidable for-mer shipyards, now home to the Museu Marítim, a good place to begin a route of waterfront Barcelona.

Proud history
Erected in 1378, enclosed by the city's 15th-century outer wall and greatly enlarged in the 17th century, the huge Drassanes launched thousands of ships. At their height they were turning out 30 war galleys at a time.

Museu Marítim
The **Museu Marítim** ❶ (Avinguda de les Drassanes; www.mmb.cat; daily 10am–8pm; charge) charts Catalonia's seafaring history with a fine collection of fishing boats and model ships, including a full-scale replica of Don Juan of Austria's victorious flagship, the *Reial*. The museum is undergoing a comprehensive remodelling. Until it re-opens at the end of 2014, there are exhibitions and activities.

Plaça Portal de la Pau
The nearby Mirador a Colom (see page 35), stands in the **Plaça Portal de la Pau** ❷ (Gate of Peace Square). It was

Rambla del Mar footbridge   *The Aquarium's glass tunnel*

through a gate on this site that Christopher Columbus triumphantly entered the city on his return from the West Indies in April 1493.

PORT VELL

Moll de les Drassanes
In front of the statue is the **Moll de les Drassanes** (*moll* means wharf), from where **Las Golondrinas ③** (Swallows) pleasure boats run trips to the entrance of the commercial harbour or to the

Olympic port (www.lasgolondrinas.com; summer daily 11.15am–8.15pm, rest of year: slightly shorter hours; charge).

To the left is the **Junta d'Obres del Port**, the Port Authority building constructed in 1907 as a reception point.

Moll de Barcelona
Today, cruise-line passengers embark at the Moll Adossat further south, but high-speed boats to the Balearics disembark at the Estació Marítim on the 500m (1,640ft) **Moll de Barcelona**.

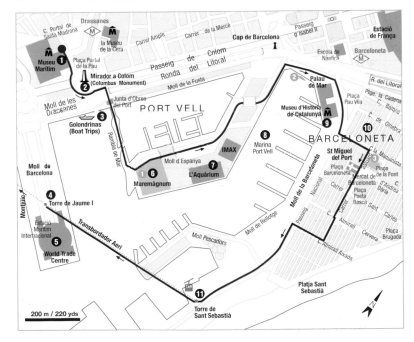

The boardwalk by Maremàgnum

The jetty also has the 119m (390ft) **Torre de Jaume I** ❹ link for the cross-harbour cable car, the **Transbordador Aeri**, erected in 1931 and leading from Montjuïc; it continues to the Torre de Sant Sebastià, at the southeastern end of the port.

At the end of the Moll de Barcelona is the **World Trade Centre** ❺, designed by architect I.M. Pei (of Paris's Louvre pyramid fame) and housing a commercial centre with offices, restaurants and a five-star hotel.

MOLL D'ESPANYA

Walk over the undulating wooden Rambla de Mar footbridge to the **Moll d'Espanya**, Port Vell's main jetty. This is a popular place for families and young Barcelonans at weekends and evenings, with the **Maremàgnum** ❻ shopping mall, Imax cinema and **L'Aquàrium** ❼ (www.aquariumbcn.com; July–Aug daily 9.30am–11pm, June and Sept 9.30am–9.30pm, Oct–May Mon–Fri 9.30am–9pm, Sat–Sun until 9.30pm; charge). In the aquarium, the blue-shimmering tanks show what swims in the surrounding seas, and a glass tunnel leads visitors among sharks and rays.

The **Maremàgnum** is home to several good refreshment options but **Tapa Tapa** provides great views while you eat, see ❶.

Outside the Imax cinema is a replica of Narcís Monturiol's wooden subma-rine, *Ictineu II*, that entered the waters here in 1864 (see box).

Moll de la Fusta and the Marina

The **Moll d'Espanya** leads ashore to the old timber wharf, the **Moll de la Fusta** (Wood Wharf), redesigned as a palm-lined promenade in the late 1980s. Where these two *molls* meet you will see the **Marina Port Vell** ❽ always bustling with yachts on the move, and here you can climb aboard the **Luz de Gas Port Vell** floating bar, see ❷. Adjacent, in the Porta del Pau, is American Pop artist Roy Lichtenstein's colourful *Cap de Barcelona* (Barcelona Head; see page 45).

> ## An idealist inventor
>
> Taking pride of place in the old port is a replica of *Ictineu II*, the world's first combustion-powered submarine. Its inventor, Narcís Monturiol (1819–85), came up with the design after witnessing the dangerous work of coral divers in Cadaqués, north of Barcelona. An idealist with socialist beliefs, Monturiol was briefly exiled to France where he met the Icarians, like-minded intellectuals who went on to try to establish Icaria, a Utopian colony in America. It failed, but the name lived on in Barcelona's industrial district, Nova Icària; this became the site of the Olympic Village, where it was hoped that Utopian values might prevail.

Yachts in the harbour   *Moll de la Barceloneta*

Museu d'Història de Catalunya
This was once a dock area that bustled with industry, but the only warehouse remaining is Elies Rogent's 1878 brick-built Magatzem General, now the Palau de Mar. Part of the building is used to house the excellent **Museu d'Història de Catalunya** ❾ (Plaça de Pau Vila 3; Tue, Thu–Sat 10am–7pm, Wed 10am–8pm, Sun 10am– 2.30pm; charge). It covers two substantial floors: the first takes the story up to the 18th century; the second begins with industrialisation and includes memories of the Franco years.

BARCELONETA

At the end of the Marina quay is **Barceloneta** ❿, once home to the city's fishing community, and created in 1753 to house citizens who had been usurped by the building of the Ciutadella fortress. The architect, military engineer Juan Martin de Cermeño, designed two-storey terraces on a grid system to allow volleys from the castle to be directed down the streets.

Though this is still a close-knit community, its small bars and restaurants have become popular with people from across the city.

In the heart of the district is a market, remodelled in 2007 by Josep Mias incorporating material from the area's 19th-century market. The market bar, **El Paco**, see ❸, is a good place to stop for snacks. Note also the Moll del Rellotge (Clock Wharf), named after the clock tower (closed to the public) that once served as a lighthouse.

Cable car ride
An option now is to continue walking for around 15 minutes to the end of the harbour and the **Torre de Sant Sebastià** ⓫. A lift ascends the iron hulk to a platform from which the cable cars fly over the harbour back to the Torre de Jaume I. Just beyond, towering above the boardwalk, is the W Barcelona hotel (see page 107).

Food and Drink

❶ TAPA TAPA
Maremàgnum Centre; floor 0, local 10; tel: 93 225 86 97; daily 11am–1am; €€€
This traditional tapas restaurant with a modern touch has a marine theme and a terrace with spectacular harbour views.

❷ LUZ DE GAS PORT VELL
Devante Palau de Mar; tel: 93 484 23 26; daily noon–3am summer only; €€
This boat, moored in the marina, is an ideal place to drop by for refreshments, for cocktails or tapas.

❸ BAR EL PACO
Mercat de Barceloneta; tel: 93 221 50 16; Mon–Thu, Sat 9am–2pm, Fri 8am–2pm, 5–10pm; €
A friendly place for coffee and snacks, or for a lunch-time menu of stuffed squid with potatoes, or rabbit in aioli.

The Arc de Triomf

CIUTADELLA

Parc de la Ciutadella is the city's favourite open space, with gardens, boating lake, museums and zoo, making a pleasant escape from the city clamour. To the north you will find the inspiring Museu de la Música and Els Encants, the bustling flea market located in the developing Plaça de les Glòries.

DISTANCE: 5km (3 miles)
TIME: 4 hours
START: Arc de Triomf
END: Plaça de les Glòries Catalanes
POINTS TO NOTE: This route could begin anywhere in the park. Its second leg could be taken by tram, or as a separate trip.

Next to the Old Town's La Ribera quarter, inland from Barceloneta, lies Parc de la Ciutadella, a large and felicitous green space. An unhurried stroll through the park may be enough of an outing, but if you feel energetic it could also be combined with a trip to the Teatre Nacional de Catalunya and the excellent Museu de la Música, as well as to the sprawling flea market of Els Encants at Plaça de les Glòries Catalanes.

ARC DE TRIOMF

On the north side of the park is the **Arc de Triomf ❶**, by the metro station of the same name. This bulky brick monument, echoing its namesake on the Champs–Élysées in Paris, was designed by Josep Vilaseca i Casanovas as the entrance to the Universal Exhibition of 1888, which was staged in the park.

Walk down the Passeig de Lluís Companys, ever-popular with men playing *petanca* (boules). The law courts are on the left, and, if you look back up the avenue, the Collserola hills provide a grand backdrop.

PARC DE LA CIUTADELLA

At the bottom of Passeig de Lluís Companys is the main entrance to the 30-hectare (75-acre) **Parc de la Ciutadella ❷** (daily 10am–sunset; free). It is easy to while away time here, in the shade of deciduous, coniferous and palm trees, all well labelled, and now inhabited by squawking parakeets.

The park takes its name from a star-shaped citadel built by Felipe V to control the city after his successful siege in 1714. The fortress was later torn down and the park given to the city to turn into a public space in 1869.

The park's Cascada fountain   *Sea lions at the zoo*

Castell dels Tres Dragons

Most of the buildings designed for the 1888 Universal Exhibition were hastily erected and not intended to last. An exception is Modernista architect Lluís Domènech i Montaner's Café-Restaurant, to the right of the park as you enter, and more often known as the **Castell dels Tres Dragons** (Castle of the Three Dragons).

This crenellated red-brick fort never opened as a restaurant but instead served as an arts-and-crafts centre and the architect's studio for a period after the exhibition closed. A parliament assembled here in 1917, and in 1934 it opened its doors to the Museu de Zoologia, now the **Laboratori de Natura ❸** (www.museuciencies.bcn.cat; closed for renovation, check for details before you visit). It will house a new research centre, plus the zoological and geological collec-

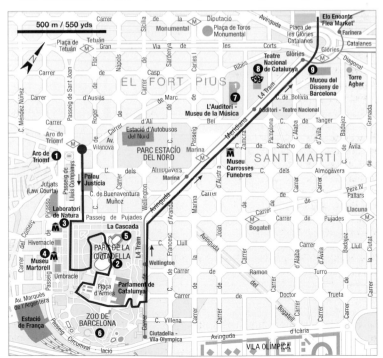

The tranquil boating lake

tions. A new natural history and science museum, the Museu Blau, opened in 2011 in the Fòrum (see page 67).

Museu Martorell

Further on is the neoclassical **Museu Martorell** (www.museuciencies. bcn.cat; closed for renovation, check for details before you visit), which was home to the city's first public museum, the former Museu de Geologia. The new museum will feature a permanent exhibition called 'A not-so-natural history: public and natural history from cabinets to museums'.

Greenhouses and water features

To either side of the Museu de Geologia lie the greenhouses of the **Hivernacle**, and the **Umbracle** palm house.

From here, cross back over the main path to **La Cascada** ⑤, a monumental fountain. The nearby Cascada Qiosc sells drinks and snacks. A few steps further on is a tranquil boating lake.

Plaça d'Armes

Beyond the lake is the **Plaça d'Armes**, where *El Desconsol* (The Inconsolable), a Josep Llimona damsel, crouches in the central pond. The buildings each side of the square are all that remain of Felipe V's citadel. Later used as a prison, the buildings were captured by Napoleon, demolished, rebuilt, handed back to the town, then bombed in the Civil War. On the west side is a chapel and, beside it, the former local governor's palace

(1748), which is now a school.

On the opposite, eastern, side of the square is the former **arsenal**, which was made into a royal palace when the park became a leisure ground in the late 19th century. This is where the **Parlament de Catalunya** sits today, guarded by the Mossos d'Esquadra, the Catalan police.

Parc Zoològic

The main avenue in the park ends at **Plaça del General Prim**, dominated by an equestrian statue of the general. This is also the entrance to the **Zoo de Barcelona** ⑥ (www.zoobarcelona.cat; daily Apr–Sept 10am–7pm, Mar and Oct 10am–6pm, Nov–Feb 10am–5pm; charge). Its Aquarama dolphin show (hourly at weekends) is the big attraction.

NORTH OF THE PARK

Exit the zoo on to **Carrer de Wellington**, where you can catch a tram up Avinguda Meridiana.

L'Auditori

Alight at the Auditori metro stop for Rafael Moneo's 1999 **L'Auditori** ⑦ (Carrer de Lepant 150; www.auditori.cat; information desk daily 8am–10pm, box office Mon–Sat 3–9pm and Sun 1 hour prior to performances; closed Aug), home to the city's resident orchestra, the Orquestra Simfònica de Barcelona y Nacional de Cataluña (OBC), with a 2,500-seat symphonic hall and a smaller space for chamber music. There is also a café, see ①.

Torre Agbar close-up

The Auditori is home to the excellent **Museu de la Música** (www.bcn.es/museumusica; Mon, Wed–Sat 10am–6pm, Sun 10am–8pm; charge). It has instruments from all over the world, with an audioguide so that you can hear what they sound like.

Teatre Nacional de Catalunya

Beside the Auditori is the vast neoclassical National Theatre, the **Teatre Nacional de Catalunya** ❽ (TNC; www.tnc.cat). Plays are generally performed in Catalan, so dance productions may be more accessible to visitors.

Plaça de les Glories Catalanes

At the top of Avinguda Meridiana is the **Plaça de les Glòries Catalanes**, an elaborate traffic junction that the architect of the Eixample originally hoped would become the new city centre. There is even a park in the middle of the junction.

A huge urban development centred on this square is well under way bringing new arts, education and health facilities to the city as well as easing traffic problems. The new state-of-the-art **Museu del Disseny de Barcelona** ❾ (www.dhub-bcn.cat) is already completed and is scheduled to open to the public in spring 2014. It will house four museums formerly in the Palau Reial (see page 83). The **Museu de Ceràmica** (www.museuceramica.bcn.es) has a collection that includes Islamic tiles, pottery by Picasso, and modern works. The three

other museums, the **Museu de les Arts Decoratives**, the **Museu Tèxtil i d'Indumentària** and the **Gabinet de les Arts Gràfiques** showcase European decorative art and Spanish industrial design, textiles and fashion from the 16th century to the present day, and graphic art and typography.

Here you will also find the new building for **Els Encants** (www.encantsbcn.com; Mon, Wed, Fri, Sat 9am–5pm; furniture auctions Mon, Wed, Fri 7.15–9am), a huge flea market, though not really a place for genuine bargains.

Torre Agbar

Towering over the area is the lipstick-shaped **Torre Agbar**, designed by the French architect Jean Nouvel, named after the water company **Aguas de Barcelona** and opened in 2005. Known locally as the Suppository, the 144m (472ft) building is Barcelona's third tallest, and features a glass facade that glows in shifting hues of red and blue at night, thanks to 4,500 led lights.

Busy bar on Platja de la Barceloneta

ALONG THE BEACH

Imported golden sand, which is cleaned daily, extends up the coast from Barceloneta, past the Port Olímpic to Poble Nou, Diagonal Mar and the Parc de Fòrum. It is ideal for a long stroll.

DISTANCE: 7km (4 miles)
TIME: 3 hours
START: Platja de Sant Sebastià
END: Fòrum
POINTS TO NOTE: In summer, this walk is best done in the morning or late afternoon to avoid the strong sun.

The curving waterfront strip covered on this route is one of the major legacies of the 1992 Barcelona Olympics. Prior to the regeneration, this was an industrial area, characterised by smoking factories and shunting yards, and in steady decline.

The whole area was planned as a smart new residential quarter, with 2,000 apartments in six-storey blocks covering 63 hectares (155 acres), and initially used as the Vila Olímpica to accommodate the competing athletes.

THE BEACHES

There are eight sections of beach along this coast, all well served with showers, bars, Creu Roja (Red Cross) emergency posts and imaginative seats from which you can catch the sun and contemplate the Mediterranean. The main railway line along the coast, serving Estació de França, is buried beneath the Ronda Litoral, which divides the beach from the buildings behind, giving the whole seafront an open, airy aspect. The promenade is popular with joggers, skaters, cyclists and walkers all year round.

Barceloneta beaches

The walk starts with the 2km (1.25-mile) **Platja de Sant Sebastià ❶** and **Platja de la Barceloneta ❷** by the fishermen's quarter (see page 59). Closest to the city centre, these busy beaches attract crowds of tourists and Barcelonans alike, and have good facilities.

Just to the northeast of Barceloneta is the **Parc de la Barceloneta ❸**, with the skeleton of an old gasometer, a Modernista warehouse, and a water tower by the Modernista architect Domènech i Estapà. Contrasting with these are the modern buildings of the Hospital del Mar. By the hospital, just before the Port

Alfredo Lanz sculpture   *Beach life*

Olímpic, walk down to the lower, beach level of the promenade, where there are several bars with sofas.

Port Olímpic

From anywhere on the beach, the **Port Olímpic ❹** (Olympic Port) is a beacon, pinpointed by Barcelona's tallest building, the Hotel Arts (see page 106) and by its neighbour, the mapfre building, housing offices. Beside them is a giant, glinting, woven-copper fish, *Pez y Esfera* (Fish and Sphere) by the architect Frank Gehry, who is best known for the Bilbao Guggenheim.

The port they overlook was built purely for leisure. Each of its quays is named after a specific wind –*Mestral*, *Xaloc* and *Gregal* (Mistral, West Wind and Northeast Wind). Yachts and dinghies set off from the quays, watched by diners in the concentration of restaurants peppered over two levels.

Beyond the port

Paella is a speciality of the beach restaurants alongside **Platja de Nova Icària ❺**, the next stretch of beach. Behind them is the Parc del Port Olímpic, a memento of the Olympics. In Plaça dels Campions (Champions' Square) are the names of the 257 gold medallists, as well as the hand prints of the footballer Pele, cyclist Eddie Merckx, chess champion Gary Kasparov and other sporting stars.

The next strip of beach is **Platja del Bogatell ❻**, hidden from the upper promenade by embankments.

POBLE NOU

Just before the Mar Bella yacht club, a line of metal poles leads inland to the **Rambla del Poble Nou ❼**, a good place for lunch or a pit stop. Try a refreshing, tiger-nut *orxata* or an ice cream at **El Tio Che**, see ❶, on the corner of Carrer del Joncar.

This is the heart of the Poble Nou district, which used to be known for its textile production. Today, the factories have been replaced by design studios, modern office towers and apartment buildings. Gentrification of the area

Street furniture

Among the most striking aspects of this city of *diseny* (design) is the carefully conceived street furniture that makes living outdoors so much more compelling. The tradition is strong. There are 1,600 public drinking fountains in the city, some designed to look like the famous Canaletes on La Rambla (see page 31), but the new ones around the Fòrum are elegant modern solutions – single corrugated sheets of metal from which water can be drawn. Seating, too, is imaginative. In the centre of the city, there is usually somewhere to sit, with single seats laid out as if in a domestic setting. Around Diagonal Mar new seats are arranged in pairs and threes beneath lamps, like sofas in a drawing room, giving the seafront a sociable air.

Shady Rambla del Poble Nou

is ongoing, spreading north and west until it eventually merges into Avinguda Diagonal.

DIAGONAL MAR

Back on the beach is **Platja de la Mar Bella** , with a sports centre behind it, and further on **Platja de la Nova Mar Bella** .

Parc de la Diagonal Mar

This immense space encapsulates the city's desire to be at the forefront of sustainable architecture. It has defined areas – a children's play area, a raised walkway over water, a lake with sculptures that spray water, curved tubular structures, a central plaza – all linked by a common element: water.

Here an urban rebirth has taken place at Diagonal Mar, a hi-tech residential and commercial neighbourhood that has brought Avinguda Diagonal, which slices diagonally through the Eixample, down to the coast. The focus of the development is the **Parc del Fòrum** , a seafront esplanade encompassing a series of buildings and amenities that stage a wide range of events, entertainments and conventions.

The landmark triangular Fòrum Building, by architects Jacques Herzog and

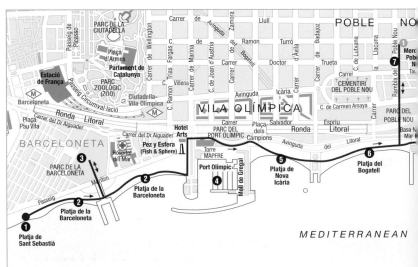

The triangular Museu Blau

Pierre de Meuron became home to the **Museu Blau** (Blue Museum; www.muscublau.bcn.cat; Tue–Sat 10am–7pm, Sun 10am–8pm; charge) in 2011. Spanning two floors, this innovative attraction takes you on a journey through the history of life on earth and is a celebration of natural sciences using interactive and audio-visual resources.

Head now towards **Plaça Fotovoltaica ⓫**, the location of a football-pitch-sized sun-catcher, with a startling skewed roof of solar panels. The indoor and outdoor auditoria are both spectacular venues for concerts.

A last stop before catching the metro or a tram (line 4) at El Maresme/Fòrum

back to the city centre is the **Marina Fòrum ⓬**, the latest harbour on this burgeoning leisure coast.

Food and Drink

❶ EL TIO CHE

Rambla del Poble Nou 44–6; tel: 93 309 18 72; www.eltioche.es; summer daily 10am–10pm, winter Tue–Sun 10am–2pm, 5–10pm; €

Operating on this site since 1933, this bar has the city's best ice creams, plus refreshing lemon slush and deliciously rich *orxata*.

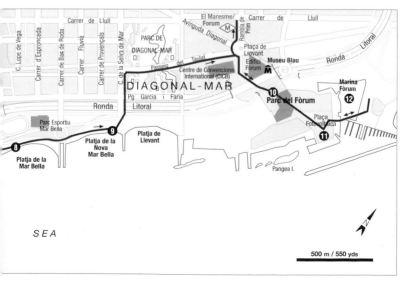

La Pedrera by night

THE EIXAMPLE

The showcase for Gaudí and the Modernista architects, the Eixample was laid out on a strict grid traversed by wide avenues. Today the fantastic facades compete for attention with stylish designer shops and chic locals.

DISTANCE: 2km (1.5 miles)
TIME: 3 hours
START/END: Passeig de Gràcia
POINTS TO NOTE: Expect queues at Gaudí's Casa Batlló and La Pedrera – book online for both or try to get there early. Note that from the end of this walk, it is only about 15 minutes' walk to the Sagrada Família (see page 72).

The Eixample (Extension) was laid out in 1860 in a grid designed by Ildefons Cerdà i Sunyer. Each block had distinct 'cut-off' corners, which offered great opportunity for a newly rich bourgeoisie to build showy homes. It is the district where there is the greatest concentration of buildings designed for domestic purposes by Antoni Gaudí and the Modernistas (see page 22), who shared the belief in craftsmanship and the importance of detail, employing masons, ceramicists, stained-glass specialists and workers in bronze and iron to transform their designs into reality.

ILLA DE LA DISCÒRDIA

The tour starts at the Passeig de Gràcia metro. Note that there are some good tapas bars on this broad avenue, see ❶ and ❷. Rambla de Catalunya, west of and parallel to Gràcia, is also very civilised, with pavement cafés and bars including **La Bodegueta**, see ❸.

Unmissable on the western side of Passeig de Gràcia, between Carrer del Consell de Cent and Carrer d'Aragó at Nos 35–43, is a trilogy of diverse Modernista works, known as **Illa de la Discòrdia** ❶ (Block of Discord), each striking in its own way.

Casas Lleó Morera and Amatller

On the southern corner of the block, at No. 35, is the privately owned **Casa Lleó Morera** (closed to the public), by Lluís Domènech i Montaner, the architect most renowned for his Palau de la Música Catalana (see page 46). The name comes from the words for 'lions' and 'mulberry trees', both elements used in the decoration. The building is distinguished by its fanciful ovoid towers.

Casa Batlló's ornate chimneys　　　　　　　　*The blue-green Casa Batlló*

Domènech i Montaner mentored Josep Puig i Cadafalch (1867–1957), architect of the next building in the trio: the Dutch-gabled, tiled **Casa Amatller**, three houses further on. The ground-floor entrance, where the caretaker's office contains one of the finest stained-glass windows of the Modernista era is open to visitors (free). There is also a gallery displaying temporary exhibitions. The house was occupied by the Amatller family (a chocolate-making dynasty) after its completion in 1900.

Casa Batlló

Next door is Gaudí's **Casa Batlló** (www.casabatllo.es; daily 9am–9pm; allow 20 minutes queuing time; best to book online; charge), with a spectacular blue-green ceramic facade, sensuously curving windows and scale-like roof reminiscent of a sea monster (some suggest it depicts St George, patron saint of Barcelona, and the dragon). The house was built for textile baron Josep Battló, from 1902–06, and its apartments, attic and roof are all now open to visitors.

FUNDACIÓ TÀPIES

After the Block of Discord, turn left into Carrer d'Aragó. At No. 255, on the north side of the street, crowned by a twisted metal sculpture entitled *Núvol i Cadira* (Cloud and Chair), is the **Fundació Tàpies** ❷ (www.fundaciotapies.org; Tue–Sun 10am–7pm). Established in 1984 by the artist Antoni Tàpies (1923–2012) and recently renovated, the foundation is part gallery – showing work by Tàpies and temporary exhibitions – and part study centre, with a smart library. It is housed in a building

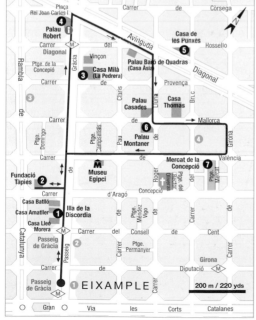

Passeig de Gràcia architecture

designed in 1880 by Lluís Domènech i Montaner for his brother's publishing company.

LA PEDRERA

Head back down Carrer d'Aragó to the Passeig de Gràcia. Cross the road and walk to the corner of Carrer de Provença, and **Casa Milà ❸** (www.lap edrera.com; daily Mar–Oct 9am–8pm, Nov–Feb 9am–6.30pm; charge), commonly called 'La Pedrera' (the stone quarry), after its rippling grey stone facade. Begun in 1901, this extraordinary edifice – Gaudí's most prominent private building – was a controversial project: an eight-storey apartment block devoid of straight lines, set around two inner courtyards. Gaudí put the city's first underground carriage park in the basement and sculpted a roof of evil-looking chimneys, inspired by medieval knights, that were dubbed *espantabruixes*, or 'witch-scarers'.

After years of neglect the building was rescued when Unesco declared it of world-heritage importance, and the Caixa de Catalunya savings bank undertook its restoration. The courtyard, attic (housing an exhibition on Gaudí's work, and of note for its fine parabolic arches), rooftop decorated with *trencadís* (mosaic of broken tiles) and a show flat, in which everything is carefully designed in the Modernista style, can all be visited. There is also a separate exhibition space for temporary shows on the first floor.

North of La Pedrera

Just beyond La Pedrera, at Passeig de Gràcia 96, is **Vinçon**, a leading interior design store, selling everything from stylish stationery and retro toys to furniture and fabrics; exhibitions are also held here. Go upstairs to appreciate the building, which was once the home of the artist Ramón Casas (1866–1932).

Nearby, at Plaça del Rei Joan Carles I, **Palau Robert ❹** houses an information centre for Catalonia. Exhibitions are held here, and there is a pleasant peaceful garden.

AVINGUDA DIAGONAL

Turn right, onto Avinguda Diagonal, which cuts the Eixample diagonally and runs down to the sea. On the right, at No.373, is the striking Modernista **Palau Baró de Quadras**, built in 1904 by Puig i Cadafalch and recently home to **Casa Àsia** cultural centre, but now part of the Institut Ramón Llull. It is not yet known if the interior will be open to public view.

As you continue down the Diagonal, look out, two blocks along, for Puig i Cadafalch's neo-Gothic **Casa de les Punxes ❺** (House of the Spikes).

Modernista landmarks

At this point turn right down Carrer de Roger de Llúria. At the corner of Carrer de Mallorca, on the northern side, is the **Palau Casades**, now housing the Il.lustre Col.legi d'Advocats (Law College). On

Casa Battló tiles *La Pedrera's undulated rooftop*

the south side is **Palau Montaner** ❻ (guided tours only Sat–Sun, tour in English Sat 10.30am; charge) with attractive tiled eaves and a mosaic exterior. Designed by Domènech i Montaner as a private home for his brother – the whole family lived here from 1893 until 1939 – it now shelters the government of Madrid in Barcelona.

Domènech i Montaner also built **Casa Thomas** at Carrer de Mallorca, 291–3, a few steps down on the left, and now occupied by Cubiña, a modern furniture designers. (You can walk in and admire the building.)

Continue a block to Carrer de Girona, then turn right and right again to the 19th-century glass-and-iron **Mercat de la Concepció** ❼ (Carrer d'Aragó 313–17; Mon, Sat 8am–3pm, Tue–Fri 8am–8pm), selling all manner of foodstuffs and with a couple of stalls where you can get a drink and a snack. Alternatively, back on Carrer de Valencia turn first right into Carrer de Bruc for lunch at **Asador de Burgos**, see ❹. On the way back to Passeig de Gràcia you will pass the **Museu Egipci** (Carrer de València 284; www.museuegipci.com; Mon–Sat 10am–8pm, Sun 10am–2pm; charge) an important private collection of Egyptian artefacts including mummies, statuary, funereal implements, ceramics and jewellery.

Food and Drink

❶ DIVINUS

Passeig de Gràcia 28; tel: 93 302 21 29; www.restaurantedivinus.com; Sun–Thu 7.30am–1.30am, Fri–Sat 9am–2am; €€
In a large, two-storey space, this excellent bar-restaurant has a slick modern feel. Traditional cooking, plus a great range of tapas.

❷ TAPA TAPA

Passeig de Gràcia 44; tel: 93 488 33 69; www.tapataparestaurant.cat; Mon–Thu 7.45am–1.30am, Fri 7.45am–2am, Sat 8.30am–2am, Sun 9.30am–1am; €€

Over 80 different tapas available in this gastronomic wonder house.

❸ LA BODEGUETA

Rambla de Catalunya 100; tel: 93 215 17 25; ww2w.labodegueta.cat; Mon–Fri 7.30am–1.45am, Sat 8am–1.45am, Sun 6.30pm–1.45am; €€
Old-fashioned bodega with big barrels and marble tables. Rough red wine accompanies *tacos de manchego* and *jamón serrano*.

❹ ASADOR DE BURGOS

Carrer de Bruc 118; tel: 93 207 31 60; www.asadordeburgos.es; daily 1–4pm, Wed–Sat also 8.45pm–11.30pm; €€
Traditional place where meat is grilled in an oak wood adobe oven.

The construction continues

SAGRADA FAMÍLIA AND PARK GÜELL

No visit to Barcelona is complete without a tour of the buildings of the great Modernista architect Antoni Gaudí. His stunning Sagrada Família is a must-see, and can be combined with a trip up to his house-museum in Park Güell.

DISTANCE: 3km (2 miles)
TIME: 4 hours
START: Sagrada Família
END: Park Güell
POINTS TO NOTE: You can buy a combined ticket for both the Sagrada Família and the Casa-Museu Gaudí in Park Güell at either place.

Start the day with the astonishing, unfinished temple of Antoni Gaudí (1852–1926), easily reached by metro. There are many places to eat on the Avinguda de Gaudí; try the traditional **La Llesca**, see ❶.

SAGRADA FAMÍLIA

After Gaudí had completed his last commission, Casa Milà (La Pedrera; see page 70), in 1910, he devoted the remaining 16 years of his life to the **Temple Expiatori de la Sagrada Família ❶** (Carrer de Mallorca 401; www.sagrada familia.cat; daily Apr–Sept 9am–8pm, Oct–Mar 9am–6pm; charge; guided tours available daily, in English; reduced price combined ticket option with Casa-Museu Gaudí in Park Güell), working unpaid from a hut on site.

Existing facades

Before entering, it is worth circling the unfinished building to get an idea of its layout. The austere west front was completed in the 1980s with statues by local artist, Josep Maria Subirachs, and by the Japanese sculptor, Etsuro Soto. The only facade Gaudí completed is the eastern one dedicated to the Nativity, with three doorways: Faith, Hope and Charity, and four coloured, tentacled towers, one of which has an internal lift to take visitors skywards.

Work in progress

Part of the fascination lies in watching the builders and craftsmen going about their work. In 2010 the main nave was finally covered, resplendent with tree-like columns and dazzling roof. The church was consecrated by Pope Benedict XVI on 7 November 2010. At 110m (360ft) in length, the Sagrada Família

The intricate interior   *Facade stonework*

will eventually be 27m (87ft) longer than the city's cathedral and nearly twice the height, with a main tower rising to 198m (650ft). The church has eight spires, with Gaudí's original plans showing 18. Completion is currently set for 2030 – the once preferred date of 2026, commemorating the centenary of Gaudí's death, now looking increasingly unlikely.

Crypt

The crypt where Gaudí is buried also houses the museum that shows how he envisaged the finished temple, and how his ideas often changed. Controversy over the final design still rages as to whether it will live up to Gaudí's dream.

HOSPITAL DE LA SANTA CREU

On leaving the Sagrada Família, stroll up Avinguda de Gaudí on the north side of the temple. This anarchic diagonal avenue leads to the **Hospital de la Santa Creu i Sant Pau ❷** (Carrer de Sant Antoni María Claret 167; tel: 93 317 76 52; guided tours in English daily 10am, 11am, noon, 1pm; charge).

Designed by Lluís Domènech i Montaner, and begun in 1902, the hospital is a fine Modernista work, with separate pavilions connected by underground walkways, in the style of a pleasant garden city. It is now a Unesco World Heritage Site.

PARK GÜELL

It is now time to progress to **Park Güell ❸** (Carrer d'Olot; www.parkguell.es; daily 8am–sunset; free). There are several ways of reaching it from the Sagrada Família: hop on the tourist bus outside the church; take the metro to Lesseps, then walk uphill 1.2km (0.75 mile) or take the No. 24 bus; or take No. 92 bus from outside the Hospital de la Santa Creu i Sant Pau. Alternatively, hail a taxi.

Casa–Museu Gaudí in Park Güell

Background

The site was originally owned by Gaudí's patron, the affluent industrialist Eusebi Güell, who had wanted to create a garden city of houses in the English style here – hence the English spelling of 'park'. The project never came to full fruition, and in 1922 the Güell family donated the park to the city instead.

The park

The main entrance is flanked by two whimsical pavilions designed by Gaudí. The one on the left is a shop, while the one on the right houses an exhibition giving the background to the construction of the park.

A double staircase, presided over by a magnificent tile-mosaic salamander, leads up to the park's main feature, a two-tiered plaza. The lower part is a hypostyle hall, originally intended to be the market hall for the estate. Framing the plaza is a wavy, tile-mosaic parapet from where there is a grand view out over the city. This long, colourful, undulating bench was actually the work not of Gaudí but his assistant, Josep Jujol i Gibert.

Casa-Museu Gaudí

In 1906, Gaudí bought the home of architect Francesc Berenguer, to the right of the park entrance. This is now the **Casa-Museu Gaudí** (www.casamuseu gaudi.org; daily Apr–Sept 10am–8pm, Oct–Mar 10am–6pm; charge), housing furniture from the architect's time, including his bed, *prie-dieu* and crucifix.

Return to the centre on bus No. 24, or from Lesseps metro.

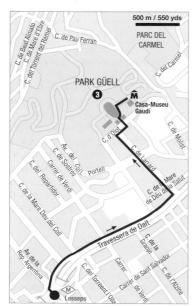

Food and Drink

❶ LA LLESCA

Avinguda de Gaudí 12; tel: 93 455 31 30; daily 1–4pm, 8.30–11.30pm; €

This family-run Catalan restaurant is good value. Its speciality dishes are braised artichokes, *escalivada* – grilled vegetables, squid Catalan-style and of course *llescas* (toasts).

The view from Palau Nacional

MONTJUÏC

Named after a Jewish cemetery, Barcelona's southern hill is home to the region's most notable art collection, a scattering of buildings erected for the 1992 Olympics, the world-class Fundació Joan Miró and the fun Poble Espanyol.

DISTANCE: 5km (3 miles)
TIME: 5 hours
START: Plaça d'Espanya
END: Paral.lel metro
POINTS TO NOTE: You will not be able to do justice to all Montjuïc's attractions in a day, so priortise before setting out. The hill is steep; take the bus or funicular to save energy.

The buildings that were erected for the 1992 Olympic Games were the last in a line of attractions to be located on the 213m (700ft) high hill of Montjuïc. The majority of the grand exhibition halls and cultural palaces here are remnants of the1929 Universal Exhibition.

But the hill has long featured in the city's history. Its stone was quarried to build the cathedral, and its castle, which has a wonderful 360-degree panorama, has witnessed all the triumphs and cruelties of the city's history.

Ongoing plans to improve and develop the Montjuïc hill include a new walkway, the Passeig del Cims (Prom-

enande of the Peaks), terraced to make climbing the steep incline easier.

One way of getting up and down Montjuïc is to use the funicular that runs from Paral.lel metro to just above the Fundació Joan Miró. From there the *teleféric* cable car ascends to the castle. The hop-on, hop-off tourist bus from Plaça d'Espanya to the castle stops at all the major sights on this route. Alternatively, hop in a taxi.

PLAÇA D'ESPANYA

The best way to approach Montjuïc, to fully appreciate its grandeur, is from the **Plaça d'Espanya ❶**. Beside the square is the neo-Mudéjar **Las Arenas**, a vast bullring built in 1899 and now home to the **Arenas de Barcelona** (www.arenas debarcelona.com) shopping centre and its theatre and concert hall, the Cúpola de las Arenas.

UP TOWARDS THE HILL

Walk up **Avinguda de la Reina Maria Cristina** through Lluís Domènech i Montaner's copies of Venice's cam-

Neoclassical Palau Nacional

panile, which flagged the triumphant approach to the 1929 exhibition. On either side of this esplanade are the vast trade fair halls of Barcelona's **Fira de Barcelona**.

Font Màgica de Montjuïc

At the top of the avenue, reached by outdoor escalators, is the **Font Màgica de Montjuïc ②** (Magic Fountain; May–Sept Thu–Sun 9–11.30pm, Oct–May Fri–Sat 7–9pm; free), designed by Carles Buïgas in 1929. Rising to 50m (164ft), it is magnificent after dark, when it is lit by 4,500 coloured lights and dances to various tunes.

Museu d'Arqueologia and around

If you were to head left at this point, you would soon reach the **Mercat de les Flors**, a complex of theatres that includes the **Institut del Teatre** and **Teatre Lliure**.

Nearby is the **Museu d'Arqueologia** (Passeig de Santa Madrona 39–41; www.mac.cat; Tue–Sat 9.30am–7pm, Sun 10am–2.30pm; charge). Built for the 1929 exhibition as the Palace of Graphic Arts, it houses archaeological finds from the city.

Opposite is a public garden leading to the open-air **Teatre Grec**. Also built for the 1929 exhibition and set in a former stone quarry, it is used for plays and

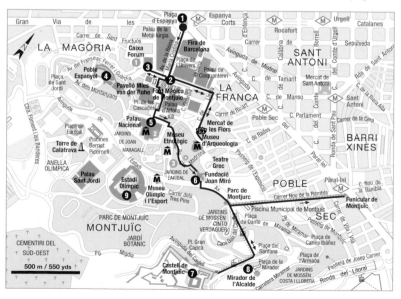

The Palau's exquisite dome *A stained-glass work at the MNAC*

concerts in the summer, as part of the two-month Festival del Grec (www.grec.bcn.cat).

Pavelló Mies van der Rohe

Back at the Font Màgica, just to its right, on Avinguda de Francesc Ferrer i Guàrdia, is the **Pavelló Mies van der Rohe** (www.miesbcn.com; daily 10am–8pm; charge). It was designed by Bauhaus director Mies van der Rohe as the German Pavilion, a reception area for the 1929 exhibition, and is remarkable for its spare lines in sleek marble and glass, complemented by a tranquil small pool. The original pavilion was demolished after the Universal Exhibition, but it was rebuilt in 1986 to celebrate the centenary of the designer's birth.

CaixaForum

Opposite the pavilion is a Modernista factory, Casaramona, built in 1911 by Josep Puig i Cadafalch. Redesigned by Arata Isozaki as the **CaixaForum ❸** (www.obrasocial.lacaixa.es; Mon–Sat 10am–8pm, Sun 10am–9pm, some areas closed Mon; free), it is one of the most exciting cultural spaces in the city, staging exhibitions across its four galleries, plus concerts, films and talks. It is also home to a permanent exhibition recounting the history of the building, a media centre, a bookshop, and a good café, see ❶.

Poble Espanyol

If you continue up Avinguda de Francesc Ferrer i Guàrdia from the CaixaForum, you will reach the ever-popular **Poble Espanyol** or Spanish Village ❹ (www.poble-espanyol.com; Mon 9am–8pm, Tue–Thu and Sun 9am–midnight, Fri 9am–3am, Sat 9am–4am; charge). Some 120 buildings represent architecture from across Spain, from Moorish Andalusia to the rugged Basque country. The complex also has a 'City of Artisans', where you can see glassmakers, weavers, potters and ironmongers at work. Its restaurants and clubs are popular in the evenings.

PALAU NACIONAL

The next main sight en route is the **Palau Nacional ❺**, the formidable neoclassical palace that dominates the fountain and the approach up Avinguda de la Reina Cristina. The palace is home to the **Museu Nacional d'Art de Catalunya** (MNAC; www.mnac.cat; Tue–Sat 10am–8pm (6pm in winter), Sun 10am–2.30pm; charge except first Sun of month; tickets are valid for two days), a repository of Catalan, Renaissance, Gothic and modern art, and, most notably, the finest collection of Romanesque art in the world.

The collection

The most striking of its lower rooms, devoted to Romanesque decoration, are those containing wall paintings peeled from the apses of remote Pyrenean churches in the early 20th century. These are complemented by crucifixes, altarpieces and caskets.

Fundació Joan Miró rooftop sculpture

The collection of Gothic and Renaissance art is less complete, although Catalonia's Gothic masters Jaume Huguet, Bernat Martorell and Lluís Borrassa are represented. The Baroque assemblage has been augmented by the addition of the Thyssen collection that was formerly housed in the Pedralbes monastery (see page 82).

The museum's Catalan collection includes 19th- and 20th-century work by Casas, Rusiñol, Gargallo and Fortuny, as well as decorative art from Modernista interiors, including furniture by Gaudí and Jujol. One room has nine works by Picasso; another is dedicated to Catalan photography, with a small collection of prints including a couple of iconic pictures from the Civil War.

In addition to the galleries, the museum houses a large concert hall, an open-plan area with comfortable sofas and a café, see ❷.

FUNDACIÓ JOAN MIRÓ

The next stop on the route is the Fundació Joan Miró, which can be reached by turning right out of the Palau Nacional and walking up the hill. This takes you past the **Museu Etnològic** (Passeig de Santa Madrona; www.museuetnologic.bcn.es; due to re-open in 2013), the city's Ethnology Museum. Turn into the lovely **Jardins de Laribal** (10am–sunset; free), where the **El Font del Gat** café-restaurant, see ❸, makes for a pleasant pit stop.

A short walk further is the **Fundació Joan Miró** ❻ (www.fundaciomiro-bcn. org; Tue–Sat July–Sept 10am–8pm, Oct–June 10am–7pm, year-round Thu until 9.30pm, Sun 10am–2.30pm; charge), in a building by architect Josep Lluís Sert (1902–83). The gallery houses a large and excellent collection of works from Joan Miró (1893–1983), including his trademark primary-colour sculptures out on the roof.

CASTELL DE MONTJUÏC

From the gallery, walk up Avinguda de Mirimar to the **funicular station**. From here, you can either take the *telefèric* cable car or a bus for the ride up to the

---

Montjuïc's gardens

There are a number of gardens on Montjuïc – the formal, French-style Jardins de Joan Maragall form the grounds of the Palauet Albéniz, while the Jardins de Mossèn Cinto Verdaguer are in the English country-house style. The 14-hectare (35-acre) Jardí Botànic, between the Olympic Stadium and the castle, is a sustainable garden showcasing plants from across the Mediterranean. Jardins de Mossèn Costa i Llobrera, on the south side of the hill and sloping towards the sea, was once a strategic defence point for the city, the Buenavista battery. The cactus garden reopened in 2011 after years of renovation.

Castell de Montjuïc   *Cable cars*

Castell de Montjuïc ❼ (tel: 93 256 44 45; daily Apr–Sept 9am–9pm, Oct–Mar 9am–7pm, free). Built in 1640 during the Harvesters' Revolt, the castle was redesigned in the reign of Felipe V. In 1939, at the end of the Civil War, it was used as a prison and execution ground. There are plans to develop the castle site in the future, possibly as a research centre promoting peace.

From just below the castle, by the **Mirador de l'Alcalde** ❽ and the statue of Sardana dancers, the *telefèric* will take you back to the funicular and Paral.lel metro, or you can get a bus back to Plaça d'Espanya.

OLYMPIC SITES

If you want to admire the legacy of the 1992 Olympic Games, take the bus that runs between the castle and the Plaça d'Espanya, and get off at the **Estadi Olímpic** ❾ (Olympic Stadium) stop. What you see today is the remodelled 1929 stadium with alterations made for the 20th European Athletics Championships, held here in 2010. It also hosts concerts.

Beside the stadium is the innovative **Museu Olímpic i de l'Esport** (www.museuolimpicbnc.cat; Apr–Sept Tue–Sat 10am–8pm, Oct–Mar 10am–6pm, Sun 10am–2.30pm all year; charge). On display are items from the 1992 Olympics and lots of interactive items and sport memorabilia.

Just beyond it are the striking **Palau Sant Jordi** indoor sports stadium and the **Bernat Picornell** swimming pools (Avinguda de l'Estadi 30; tel: 93 423 40 41; outdoor pool: June–Sept Mon–Fri 9.30am–8.30pm, Sat 9.30am–8pm, Sun 10.30am–7pm, Oct–May Mon–Sat 10am–6pm, Sun 10am–4pm; indoor pool longer hours; charge). With precipitous tiered seating, they have fabulous views of the city.

The 188m (616ft) **Torre de Calatrava** communications tower rises from the **Plaça d'Europa**, from where there are fine views to the south.

Food and Drink

❶ CAIXAFORUM

Avinguda del Marqués de Comillas 6–8; tel: 93 476 86 69; Sun–Fri 10am–6pm, Sat 10am–10pm; €
A daily set menu, plus salads, sandwiches, pastries and juices.

❷ CAFÉ DEL MNAC

Palau Nacional; tel: 93 622 03 60; Tue–Sat 10am–6pm, Sun–Mon 10am–3pm; €
A slice of the Oval Hall is taken up with this straightforward café serving sandwiches and pastries.

❸ EL FONT DEL GAT

Passeig de Santa Madrona 28; tel: 93 289 04 04; Tue–Sun 10–5pm; €€
This café-restaurant offers home-made ices and sorbets, and a good fixed-price lunch menu.

A Barça supporter's essentials

BARÇA

One of the world's richest football clubs, with about 170,000 members, and Barcelona's top team, Barça infuses the city with pride. Its museum, the focus of this short route, is one of the most popular in the city.

> **DISTANCE:** 1km (0.5 mile)
> **TIME:** 2 hours
> **START/END:** Palau Reial metro
> POINTS TO NOTE: There are very few cafés or restaurants in the vicinity of Camp Nou so consider eating elsewhere before your visit or bring a packed lunch with you.

After the Museu Picasso, the museum at Barça football club is the most visited in the city. Fans from all over the world come to see one of Europe's largest stadiums, to wonder at the club's many trophies, gloat over past glories and stand in the director's box. Barça matches bring the city to a standstill and have Barcelonans in thrall.

Getting there

When you step out of the **Palau Reial metro ❶** on the south side of Avinguda Diagonal, the dome of the stadium is immediately evident behind the massive university car park. It is just a 10-minute walk through the car park to the entrance, where stalls sell souvenir scarves, strips and other memorabilia. But wait till you get inside the wire fence to find the largest collection of memorabilia, in the two-storey **FC Botiga Megastore**.

CAMP NOU STADIUM

The stadium, **Camp Nou ❷** (Avinguida de Aristides Maillol, Les Corts; www.fcbarce

---

More than a club

The Barça slogan, *'més que un club'* (more than a club), reflects the club's place in the cultural history of Catalonia. It presents Barça as the defender of rights and freedoms, a reputation earned during the Franco years, when matches against Madrid were notoriously weighted in the capital's favour. Today, Barça's fan base extends well beyond Catalonia, and to show its continued caring side towards the world, it makes a regular contribution to United Nations' humanitarian aid programmes, and players wear the Unicef logo on the back of their shirts.

Barça's slogan

Interactive attractions at Camp Nou

lona.com; Apr–Sept Mon–Sat 10am–8pm, Sun 10am–2.30pm, Oct–Mar Mon–Sat 10am–6.30pm, Sun 10am–2.30pm, some seasonal variations; charge), meaning 'new ground', has been home to the club since 1957. It is the largest constituent part of a sports complex just below the university campus and the smart end of Avinguda Diagonal and can hold around 99,000 spectators.

Basketball, hockey, handball, junior football and ice hockey are also catered for in its neighbouring buildings, the **Miniestadi**, the **Palau Blaugrana** and the **Pista de Gel** ice rink.

Tour and museum

The main ticket office, opposite the store, is where to buy tickets to the **Museu del FC Barcelona** (opening hours as above). The entrance fee includes an audio tour of the dressing rooms, tunnel to the pitch, players' benches, presidential box and press room. There are multimedia displays and of course the many trophies Barça has amassed in its illustrious history. There is a roll-call of famous players and managers, and action-replay videos. The best part, however, is simply looking out on to the breathtaking arena and imagining the mood during games.

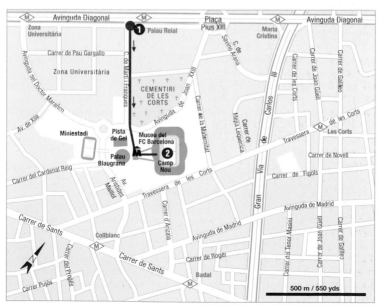

Palau Reial, Pedralbes

PEDRALBES

*This tour starts in the genteel suburb of Sarrià, then heads to the atmospheric
Gothic monastery of Pedralbes in the hills and, further down, the 20th-century
Palau Reial, which has a fabulous ceramics collection.*

DISTANCE: 2km (1 mile)
TIME: 3 hours
START: Reina Elisenda FGC station, Sarrià
END: Palau Reial metro
POINTS TO NOTE: The FGC train from Plaça de Catalunya takes 10 minutes to Sarrià (bus takes 40 minutes), from where it is a 10-minute walk to the monastery, then 20 minutes on foot to the Palau Reial. Take water with you, as there are few cafés en route.

Reina Elisenda FGC station is in the centre of **Sarrià** ❶, once a village,

Food and Drink

❶ CASA JOANA

Carrer Major de Sarrià 59, Sarrià; tel: 93 203 10 36; Mon–Sat 1–4pm, 9–11pm; €

Long-established, little-changed place, serving tasty home cooking at good prices.

now an atmospheric, sought-after district of Barcelona, with a market, smoky bars and traditional restaurants, see ❶. The *barrio* is somewhat reminiscent of a provincial Catalan town, with gardens bursting with bougainvillea, pretty Modernista villas and old-fashioned shops.

THE MONASTERY

From the station, walk along Passeig de la Reina Elisenda de Montcada to the gold-stoned **Monestir de Pedralbes** ❷ (Baixada del Monestir 9; tel: 93 256 34 34; Apr–Sept Tue–Fri 10am–5pm, Sat 10am–7pm, Sun 10am–8pm, Oct–Mar Tue–Fri 10am–2pm, Sat–Sun 10am–5pm; charge except first Sun of month), accessed up a cobbled lane and through an arch.

The monastery was founded by Queen Elisenda de Montcada, wife of Jaume II (the Just), for nuns of the Order of St Clare. The queen took the vows and retreated here after Jaume's death in 1327. There are still a few nuns living here, but most parts of the monastery

Monestir de Pedralbes

are open to visitors as the **Museu Monestir de Pedralbes**.

The three-storey clolster ls Catalan-Gothic at its most elegant. Former nuns' cells lead off around the sides.

When the monastery was fully operational, the sick were tended in the infirmary, and four rooms from this part of the complex now contain exhibits on the daily routine of the Poor Clares who lived here. You can visit the refectory where they ate in silence.

The church

Leaving the museum, continue along the side of the building to reach the entrance to the complex's church, a simple Gothic building containing Queen Elisenda's marble tomb.

FINCA GÜELL

Leave the monastery and walk down Avinguda de Pedralbes, past the luxurious apartment blocks in this exclusive part of town. Near the bottom, on the former farm estate of Gaudí's patron, Eusabi Güell, you will see, at No. 7, the **Pavellons de la Finca Güell ❸** (www.rutadelmodernisme.com; open for guided visits only; tours in English Sat–Sun 10.15am and 12.15pm; charge) with a magnificent entrance gate, a tortuous iron work by Gaudí featuring a dragon known as the Drac de Pedralbes.

PALAU REIAL

Beyond the Finca, accessed from Avinguda Diagonal, the Renaissance-style **Palau Reial ❹** (Avinguda Palau Reial de Pedralbes), surrounded by formal Italianate gardens, was built by the city council in 1925 to encourage visits from Alfonso XIII (his throne room is still here).

Return to the city centre via the Palau Reial metro just outside the palace entrance.

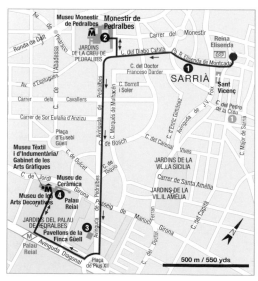

Casa Vicens

GRÀCIA

Away from the bustle of the town centre, the slightly bohemian neighbourhood of Gràcia offers peaceful streets, some with lovely Modernista facades, intriguing shops and bars, and a sense of community.

DISTANCE: 2km (1 mile)
TIME: 1hr 30mins
START: Fontana metro
END: Diagonal metro
POINTS TO NOTE: This is a suggested walk around Gràcia, but there are few key monuments in this area.

Above the Diagonal, beyond the Passeig de Gràcia, the *vila* of Gràcia was, until 1897, a community in its own right. With a reputation for radicalism and a strong identity, it maintains a tradition of artisans and small family businesses. It is full of lovely cafés and bars and attractive little squares. At night, as doors open on bars, restaurants, as well as a theatre with a strong local reputation, the area has a more vibrant ambience.

CASA VICENS

Start at the **Fontana metro ❶** in **Carrer Gran de Gràcia**, an extension of the Passeig de Gràcia, lined with shops and Modernista apartment blocks and also

El Cafè del Sol on Plaça del Sol   *Street art in Gràcia*

the location of one of Barcelona's finest fish restaurants, **Botafumeiro**, see ❶. The Modernista facades are even more striking in **Rambla del Prat**.

At the end of the Rambla turn right, then take the second right down Carrer de les Carolines, and you will see **Casa Vicens** ❷, on the left. This was Antoni Gaudí's first major commission, from a ceramic and tile manufacturer – as is evident from the colourful facade. Closed to the public, the building has been inhabited by the same family since 1885.

PLAÇA DEL SOL

Continue across Gran de Gràcia, turn right and zigzag down the small streets, lined with workshops, grocery stores and trendy clothes shops, until you reach **Plaça del Sol** ❸, lined by cafés, including the ever-popular **Sol Soler**, see ❷. The square becomes a centre of the area's night-time buzz.

Attractive architecture includes the green *esgrafiat* (incised decoration) on the Envalira restaurant, while a Lebanese restaurant in the square is a sign of the growing social mix.

PLAÇA DE LA VILA DE GRÀCIA

Continue down, across the lively Travessera de Gràcia, home to the local market, to Gràcia's main square, **Plaça de la Vila de Gràcia** ❹, formerly called Plaça de Rius I Taulet and renamed in

2009. Highlights include **El Rellotge**, the 1864 town hall clock tower.

Wend your way towards the bottom of Gran de Gràcia and **Casa Fuster** ❺, Domènech i Montaner's last building in Barcelona, completed in 1911. Built over six storeys with marble columns and luxuriant stone carving, it was the most expensive private building in the city. For many years the Café Vienès occupied the ground floor, and El Danubio dance hall was in the basement. In 2000 the building was purchased by the Hoteles Center company and overhauled as a magnificent 5-star hotel, and the Café Vienès reopened on the ground floor.

From here it is just a short walk down to Avinguda Diagonal and the Diagonal metro.

Food and Drink

❶ BOTAFUMEIRO

Carrer Gran de Gràcia 81; tel: 93 218 42 30; www.botafumeiro.es; daily noon–1am; €€€€

One of the best (and most expensive) fish restaurants in Barcelona. So good even the king has dined here.

❷ SOL SOLER

Plaça del Sol 21; tel: 93 217 44 40; daily noon–1am; €€

This old bodega has wooden tables and a lively young crowd. Simple food includes couscous, *tortillas* and quiche.

Looking down from Tibidabo

TIBIDABO

The hill that looks down on Barcelona is crowned by a historic amusement park and criss-crossed by walking paths. It is accessible by tram and funicular, with the excellent CosmoCaixa science museum en route.

DISTANCE: 10km (6 miles)
TIME: 5 hours
START: Avinguda Tibidabo FGC
END: Plaça de Catalunya
POINTS TO NOTE: Tibidabo funfair is open from March to December only. The best time to visit is late afternoon or early evening, as the sunsets are spectacular. The Tramvia Blau and funicular only run when the Parc d'Atraccions is open.

According to the Bible, the Devil took Christ up into 'an exceeding high mountain and sheweth him all the kingdoms of the world, and the glory of them; and saith unto him, All these things *I will give thee* [*tibi dabo*] if thou wilt fall down and worship me.'

Tibidabo is the 517m (1,700ft) summit of the Collserola hills behind the city. With the haze caused by city traffic there is usually a fine view only of the skyline, but on rare occasions the view reaches across Barcelona to the sea, the Balearic Islands, north to the Pyre-nees and west to Montserrat.

An afternoon or evening out at these dizzy heights can be a family occasion, starting with hands-on fun at Cosmo-Caixa, Barcelona's science museum, before continuing up the hill to take in the Tibidabo amusement park.

TRAMVIA BLAU

Getting up the hill is part of the fun. Take the FGC train to **Avinguda Tibidabo ❶** station, then cross Passeig de Sant Gervasi. Here, at the beginning of Avinguda del Tibidabo, is the stop for the old-fashioned, open-sided wooden **Tramvia Blau** (Blue Tram) that will take you to the funicular that goes up to Tibidabo every 30 minutes. The tram is part of the original Barcelona tram system and in 2011 celebrated 100 years in operation. The more frequent No. 196 bus, which leaves from the stop a few steps further on, also goes to the fun park. During summer months the T2 Tibibus will take you all the way from Plaça Catalunya to the park.

CosmoCaixa science museum   *Avion Tibiair at the Parc d'Atraccions*

Avinguda del Tibidabo

The ride up this grand avenue takes you past Modernista houses and villas, built for the city's elite intent on escaping the hassle of industrial Barcelona, and characterised by lavish turrets and tiles. The villa at No. 31 is now the smart **El Asador de Aranda**, see ❶.

COSMOCAIXA

Part way up the hill, en route to the funicular (about 15 minutes' walk or two stops on bus No. 60) is the science museum, **CosmoCaixa** ❷ (Carrer de Isaac Newton 26; www.obrasocial.lacaixi.es; Tue–Sun 10am–8pm; charge). Situated on the left just before the Ronda de Dalt highway, it is one of the most entertaining museums in the city.

There are numerous interactive exhibits, including energy and force machines, and computers to test reflexes, equilibrium, colour awareness and ability to lie. There are also microscopes and satellite pictures, even a submarine. Click and Flash, an area aimed at 3- to 6-year-olds, was created by designer Xavier Mariscal to give little ones their first taste of science, through stimulating interactive displays. The Planetarium, projects a stereoscopic 3D effect, using the latest technology to immerse viewers in the action.

When you have finished at the museum, continue up the hill towards the funicular, or return to the bus stop, if you can't face the walk.

Drinks with a view

Once across the Ronda de Dalt, the road winds through bosky estates peppered with Modernist fantasies until it reaches the funicular station at Plaça del Doctor Andreu. Here, there is a choice of places to

Sagrat Cor

stop for a drink with great views over the city, including **La Venta**, see ❷, and **Mirablau**, see ❸.

The funicular

The Art Deco funicular, which opened in 1901, runs to the top of Tibidabo, taking seven minutes to ascend its almost vertical track. Choose whether to buy a single or return ticket (a return is slightly cheaper than two singles). If you fancy a 30-minute bus ride back to Plaça de Catalunya from the top – or a walk down – plump for a single.

The Collserola hills

The Collserola park, on the other side of the hill from the funfair, is a great place for walks, cycling or picnics. A mere 13-minute train ride from Plaça de Catalunya through a tunnel takes you to Baixador de Vallvidrera. Here you step out into another world, with the pine-scented air hitting you as soon as the doors open. Walk up the landscaped path to the information centre (www.parcnaturalcollserola.net; 10am–3pm), a helpful base, with maps, advice, an exhibition on wildlife, and a bar/restaurant. Close by is the atmospheric Villa Joana (Casa-Museu Verdaguer) (tel: 93 204 78 05; Sat–Sun 10am–2pm; free), where the much-loved poet Jacinct Verdaguer lived until his death in 1902. Footpaths lead into the woods with *fonts* (natural springs) and picnic spots.

PARC D'ATRACCIONS

The **Parc d'Atraccions** ❸ (Plaça del Tibidabo; www.tibidabo.cat; Aug Wed–Sun noon–11pm, July Wed–Fri noon–9pm, Sat–Sun noon–10pm, Mar–June Sat–Sun noon–7pm, Sept–Oct noon–9pm, Nov–Dec noon–6pm; charge; all-in tickets permit unlimited access to the rides), dating back to 1901, is one of the oldest amusement parks in the world. With over 25 rides, street shows, theatre and other entertainment for all ages, the park can take a good few hours to explore properly. Many of the old favourites remain but there is now a new generation of theme-park rides. The majority are still fairly tame but La Muntanya Russa, a head-spinning roller-coaster, and Avion Tibiair are both likely to give you an adrenalin rush. Check out the Sky Walk, an area with the best views of Barcelona. There is also a **Museu de Automàts**, with mechanical toys from the first half of the 20th century.

THE SAGRAT COR

There is more to Tibidabo than the funfair – there are restaurants with panoramic views, including **La Masia** and the **Gran Hotel La Florida**, see ❹, and ❺, and pleasant paths to walk. Many people come here to visit the **Sagrat Cor** (Plaça del Tibidabo; www.templotibidabo.info; daily 10.30am–3pm, 4–7pm; charge), the Sacred Heart church, a bulky 20th-century architectural confection on the

'Torre Foster'   Viewpoint at the Torre de Collserola

site of a chapel used by the hermit Joan Bosco, in the 19th century. There is a lift in the tower up to the top from where there are marvellous views of the city. The original chapel can be seen behind the main church.

TORRE DE COLLSEROLA

At this point you may wish to return to the city, but if you are up for an even more spectacular view, go down the road behind the Hotel La Masia to the **Torre de Collserola** ❹ (www.torrecollserola. com; same hours as Parc d'Atraccions;

charge), which you will undoubtedly have seen ever since your arrival on Tibidabo. You can take the lift to the glassed-in observation platform on the 10th floor of the 288m (945ft) communications tower. Designed by British architect Norman Foster for the 1992 Olympics, it is sometimes known as **Torre Foster**.

If you wanted to return a different way, a 20-minute walk will take you to the Modernista funicular station of **Vallvidrera Superior**. The funicular takes you down to the fgc station at **Peu del Funicular**, from where it is only a 15-minute train ride back to Plaça de Catalunya.

Food and Drink

❶ EL ASADOR DE ARANDA
Avinguda del Tibidabo 31; tel: 93 417 01 15; www.asadordearanda.com; Mon–Sat 1–4pm, 9pm–midnight; €€€
The flagship of this high-quality chain of restaurants serves hearty Castilian food. The house speciality is lamb roasted in a clay oven.

❷ LA VENTA
Plaça del Doctor Andreu s/n; tel: 93 212 64 55; www.restaurantelaventa.com; Tue–Sun 1.30–3.30pm, 9–11.30pm; €€€
Stylish bar and Catalan restaurant.

❸ MIRABLAU
Plaça del Doctor Andreu 2; tel: 93 418 58 79; www.mirablaubcn.com; Mon–Thur

11am–4am, Fri–Sun 11am–5am; €€€
Restaurant and cocktail lounge with a terrace and stunning views.

❹ RESTAURANT LA MASIA
Plaça del Tibidabo 3–4; tel: 93 417 63 50; daily 10.30am–8pm; €€
Specialising in Catalan cuisine, La Masia has a glazed veranda with fine views over the city.

❺ GRAN HOTEL LA FLORIDA
Carretera de Vallvidrera al Tibidabo 83–93; tel: 93 259 30 00; www.hotellaflorida.com; restaurant: Tue–Sat 7–11am, 1–3.30pm, 8.30–11pm, Mon 7–11am, 1–3.30pm only; €€€
Opened in 1925, this grand venue has now been revitalised. You can eat at L'Orangerie, the lovely restaurant, or just drop in for a drink at the bar.

The beach at Sitges

SITGES

Just 40km (25 miles) south of Barcelona and generally sunnier, the elegant seaside town of Sitges has a rich artistic heritage, having long attracted painters, writers and other creative people. Since the 1960s, it has been the focal point of the gay scene on this stretch of coastal northeastern Spain.

DISTANCE: 40km (25 miles) one way
TIME: A full day
START: Sitges train station
END: Cementiri de Sant Sebastià
POINTS TO NOTE: Regular trains to Sitges run from Passeig de Gràcia or Sants stations (line C2; around 40 minutes). By car, the C32 motorway has been blasted through the Garraf mountains to alleviate the congested motorway. Don't forget your swimming costume.

The best known of the coastal resorts within easy reach of Barcelona, Sitges is an attractive, cosmopolitan place with excellent shops, great restaurants and a buzzing gay scene.

The making of a resort

A former wine town that had trade links with America, Sitges prospered in the 19th century, when so-called *americanos*, local people who had found fortune abroad, came home to retire in mansions and build summer houses.

The Luminist School of Sitges, comprising artists such as Joan Roig i Soler and Arcadi Mas i Fontdevila, were attracted by the superior quality of light in this seaside town in the second half of the 19th century. However, when *fin-de-siècle* Modernista artist and writer Santiago Rusiñol (1861– 1931) bought a home here in 1891, Sitges was dubbed 'the Mecca of Modernisme' by the Barcelona press, and Rusiñol was credited with having discovered the place.

The resort's popularity with the bohemian crowd continued: Spanish poet and playwright Federico García Lorca (1899–1936) stayed here, as did the French composer Erik Satie (1866– 1925) and the English writer G.K. Chesterton (1874–1936).

In the late 1950s and early 1960s Sitges responded to the flood of tourists to the coast with pubs, bars and a few hotels; local people rented out rooms in summer, and a few entrepreneurs built modest apartment blocks. It was at this point that the town began to attract the gay community.

Enjoying the waves	*Perfecting that tan*

TOWARDS THE OLD TOWN

As you exit from **Sitges station ❶** you will pass the renovated municipal **Mercat** (Mon–Sat 8.30am–2pm, also Tue, Thur, Fri 5.30–8.30pm). If you want to eat while you are in the vicinity of the station, two recommendations for food are **Reves**, see **①**, and **El Celler Vell**, see **②**.

From the station, all roads seem to lead down to the sea. The first three cross Carrer de Sant Gaudenci and lead to **Plaça Cap de La Vila ❷**, the heart of the pedestrianised shopping area, with numerous cafés and bars spilling on to the street.

Left of here, on Carrer d'Angel Vidal, is the **Pati Blau**, a recreation of a painting of a blue courtyard by Rusiñol. Straight ahead is Carrer Major, which takes you down to the old town.

MUSEU ROMÀNTIC

At this point, however, our recommendation is a detour to the right down Carrer de Parallades, a busy shopping street, then first right into Carrer de Sant Gaudenci for the **Museu Romàntic ❸** (Casa Llopis, Carrer de Sant Gaudenci 1; www. museusdesitges.com; July–Sept Tue–Sun 11am–8pm, Oct–June 10am–2pm,

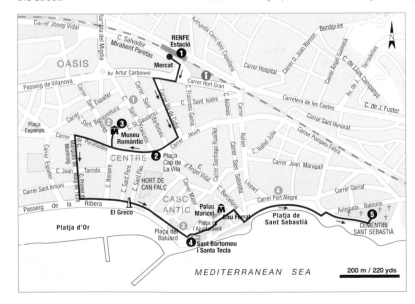

View over the town

3.30pm–7pm, Sun 11am–3pm; charge). This house, built in 1793 by the cultured Llopis family, was given to the town as a museum of family life. On the top floor is a large collection of antique dolls amassed by local children's writer Lola Anglada (1893–1984).

CARRER DEL PECAT

Continue down Carrer de Parallades to Carrer del Marqués de Montroig and turn left into Carrer Primer de Maig de 1838. This is the main pedestrian avenue running down to the sea, lined with bars and popularly known as the Street of Sin, **Carrer del Pecat**.

This is the focal point for some of the largest events in Sitges' busy festive calendar. At Corpus Christi (in June), the street is covered in a carpet of flowers, while during the pre-Lent carnival parade, there is an elaborate show of costume and design here. The Shrove Tuesday evening parade is probably the town's most outrageous spectacle, with the glamour hitting top notes at the transvestite festival.

THE BEACH

At the bottom of the street is the palm-fringed promenade Passeig de la Ribera, which is lined by the gently curving **Platja d'Or**, a golden strand some 5km (3 miles) long. For an up-market lunch, continue to the left, towards the end of the beach promenade to **Fragata**, see ❸.

PALAU MARICEL

The beach ends just beyond the monument to the painter El Greco on the rocky promontory that is dominated by the 17th-century church of **Sant Bartomeu i Santa Tecla ❹**.

Just behind the church, in Carrer Fonollar, are some magnificent white mansions and, on the left at Nos 2–6, the **Palau Maricel** (tel: 93 894 03 64; for tours call for details), with a lovely blue-tiled roof terrace. The palace was built in 1910 by the American philanthropist Charles Deering (1852–1927) to house his art collection (sadly now dispersed).

Deering also purchased the building opposite, a former hospital dating from the 14th century, and connected it to his own palace by an overhead passageway. The hospital now houses the **Museu Maricel** (Carrer Fonollar; tel: 93 894 03 64; closed for renovation, due to reopen summer 2014; charge), with a fine collection of Gothic paintings and furniture and a room decorated by Josep Luís Sert. This is also the home of the town's main art collection, with works by the Romantics, Luminists and Modernistas who were associated with Sitges.

SANTIAGO RUSIÑOL

The neighbouring building is home to the **Museu Cau Ferrat** (Carrer Fonollar; www.mnac.es; closed for renovation; charge), erstwhile home of the painter

Festival celebrations

Santiago Rusiñol and now the show-case for his collection, including two El Grecos, five small Picassos and works by Casas.

Like many artists of his generation, Rusiñol was funded by his family, which had grown rich thanks to Barcelona's industrial revolution. Rusiñol travelled frequently to Paris, forging important links for local artists. He purchased fishermen's cottages in Sitges, which he converted into a mansion to house his collection of ironwork, sculptures and paintings and to use as a studio. Between 1892 and 1899 he also organised the Festes Modernistes, a music and drama festival.

SANT SEBASTIÀ BEACH

North of these imposing buildings is **Platja de Sant Sebastià**. Quieter than the main beach, it offers good restaurants, including **Costa Dorada**, scc ❹, and pavement cafés.

If it is not too hot, or if you tire of the beach, an option is to head up the scrubby paths on the far side of Platja de Sant Sebastià towards the atmos-pheric **Cementiri de Sant Sebastià** ❺ (Avingata Balmins; tel: 93 706 57 28; summer Mon–Sat 9am–1pm, 3–6pm, Sun 9am–1pm, winter Mon–Sat 8am–1pm, 3–5pm, Sun 9am–1pm; 1 Nov 8am–6pm; free), the town's cemetery.

Food and Drink

❶ REVES

Carrer de Sant Francesc 35;
tel: 93 894 76 25; Tue–Sat 1.30–4.30pm, 8.30–11.30pm; €€
Attractive restaurant/tapas bar featuring the local speciality *xató de sitges* (salad with anchovies, tuna and salt cod).

❷ EL CELLER VELL

Carrer Sant Bonaventura 21; tel: 93 811 19 61; www.elcellervell.com; Fri–Tue 1–3.30pm, 8.15–11pm, Thur 8.15–11pm; €€
This old cellar serves good traditional Catalan cooking: grilled meats and fish and

specials such as rabbit with artichokes. Good value set meals too.

❸ FRAGATA

Passeig de la Ribera 1; tel: 93 894 10 86; www.restaurantefragata.com; daily 12.30–4pm, 8.30pm–12.30am; €€€€
This unfussy restaurant serves top-notch seafood specialities, and meat dishes, too.

❹ COSTA DORADA

Carrer Port Alegre 27; tel: 93 894 35 43; www.restaurantecostadorada.com; Fri–Tue 1–4.30pm, 8–11pm, Wed 8–11pm); €€€
On a quieter stretch of the seafront, this bright, airy restaurant has been in the same family since 1968. There is an emphasis on fresh seafood, and it's a good place to try *xató*.

Stained-glass window, Museu del Vi, Vilafranca

WINE TOUR

Catalonia is a major wine-producing region, known for its cava, an inexpensive, earthy, non-acidic sparkling drink. A tour of the Penedès region gives you a chance to see some lovely countryside as well as tasting various delicious wines.

DISTANCE: 55km (35 miles)
TIME: A full day
START: Sant Sadurní d'Anoia
END: Vilafranca
POINTS TO NOTE: Take the train from Barcelona Sants or Plaça de Catalunya (Line 4; 45 mins). Vilafranca is on the same line, just 10–15 mins further. By car, take the A2/A7 motorway from Barcelona (direction Tarragona).

Around 90 percent of the country's cava output comes from the Penedès region, south of Barcelona, in vineyards around the town of Sant Sadurní d'Anoia. Catalonia's main wine town is nearby Vilafranca del Penedès.

SANT SADURNÍ D'ANOIA

Freixenet

Beside the station at **Sant Sadurní d'Anoia** ❶ is **Freixenet** (Carrer de Joan

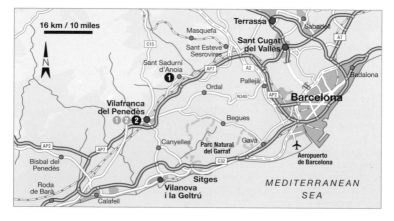

Cellars at Freixenet

Sala 2; www.freixenet.es; Mon–Sat 10am–6pm, Sun 10am–2.30pm, seasonal variations; charge), one of the largest producers in the region. There are regular 90-minute tours of the cellars with tastings.

Codorníu

Even more impressive is the original home of cava, **Codorníu** (Avinguda de Jaume Codorníu; www.codorniu.com; pre-arranged tours only; charge), about 20 minutes' walk (signposted) from the station. Josep Raventós, of the Codorníu family dynasty, popped the first cava cork here in 1872, and his son Manuel added the huge Modernista cellars, designed by Puig i Cadafalch, from 1902–15. The cellars are now a national monument. Tours include an explanation of the wine-making business, a tour of the museum and a train ride through the vast cellars.

VILAFRANCA

Opportunities for lunch in Sant Sadurní are limited, so best to continue to **Vilafranca del Penedès ②**, slightly further down the railway line (also on the A7). There are some excellent restaurants here, including **Cal Ton**, see ①, and the traditional **Casa Joan**, see ②.

Wall tiles in the Plaça de la Villa in Vilafranca celebrate the *castellers*. These human towers are attempted at the end of August as teams, physically supported by the crowds, compete for height, balance and skill.

Torres

All the bars bear the motto *Hi ha Cava a copes* (There is cava by the glass here), but Vilafranca is actually the centre for still-wine production. The old bodega of the great **Torres** family is at Carrer de Comercio 22, beside the station. You can also visit their state-of-the-art winery at **Pacs** (www.torres.es; Mon–Sat 9.15am–4.45pm, Sun 9.15am–1pm; charge), just outside the town.

Vinseum

Spain's best wine museum, **Vinseum** (Plaça de Jaume I 1; tel: 93 890 05 32; Tue–Sat 10am–2pm, 4–7pm, Sun 10am–2pm; charge includes tasting and audio guide) occupies a former royal palace. The museum showcases wine-making implements and the region's wine.

Food and Drink

① CAL TON

Carrer de Casal 8, Vilafranca del Penedès; tel: 93 890 37 41; www.restaurantcalton. com; Tue–Sat 1–4pm, 8.30–10.30pm, Sun 1–4pm; €€€
Chef Toni Mata's innovative Catalan cooking uses the best local ingredients.

② CASA JOAN

Plaça de l'Estació 8; Vilafranca del Penedès; tel: 93 890 21 71; Mon–Sat 1–4pm; €€
Superb Catalan dishes and desserts.

Exterior of the Teatre-Museu Dalí in Figueres

DALÍ TOUR

The Surrealist artist Salvador Dalí was born and lived in the Empordà region, where his museum, home and the castle he gave to his wife Gala – the 'Dalí Triangle' – are worthy legacies of his eccentricity and talent.

DISTANCE: 80km (50 miles)
TIME: At least a full day
START: Figueres
END: Port Lligat or Púbol
POINTS TO NOTE: The Teatre-Museu Dalí in Figueres is accessible by train from Barcelona and Dalí's house in Port Lligat by bus. To get to the Castell Gala-Dalí at Púbol, you need a car.

FIGUERES

Salvador Dalí was born in 1904 in the pleasant market town of **Figueres ❶** some 24km (15 miles) from the French border. Here he founded a permanent home for his work at **Teatre-Museu Dalí** (Plaça Gala-Salvador Dalí 5; www.salvadordali.org/museus/figueres; July–Sept daily 9am–8pm, Mar–June and Oct 9.30am–6pm, Nov–Feb 10.30am–6pm, closed Mon Oct–May; charge), opened in 1974. The adjacent Torre Galatea (named after Gala), added in 1981, is where Dalí died in 1989. He is buried in the museum's crypt.

The collection

Among the extraordinary works here are the *Poetry of America*, or *Cosmic Athletes*, painted in 1943, a portrait of Gala as Leda (the swan), and the huge ceiling fresco in the Wind Palace Room. In the garden, the *Rainy Cadillac* sculpture is a crowd puller. In the adjoining annexe is the dazzling exhibition of Dalí's jewels.

A good place to eat in Figueres is the **Hotel Empordà**, see ❶.

Food and Drink

❶ HOTEL EMPORDÀ

Avenida Salvador Dalí i Domènech 170; Figueres; tel: 972 50 05 62; www.hotelemporada.com; daily 7.30–11am, 12.45–3.45pm, 8.30–10.45pm; €€€
A pioneer of the Catalan *nouvelle cuisine*.

❷ HOTEL PORT LLIGAT

Port Lligat; tel: 972 25 81 62; www.portlligat.net/hotel; Apr–Sept daily 1.30–3pm, 8.30–10pm; €€
Pleasant café opposite Dalí's house.

Spectacular ceiling fresco at the Teatre-Museu Dalí

PORT LLIGAT

From Figueres it is around 40km (25 miles) east on the C260 and GI614 to the seaside town of **Cadaqués**.

Casa-Museu Dalí

Located in the next cove, is **Port Lligat**  and the seafront **Casa-Museu Dalí** (Port Lligat; www.salvador-dali.org/museus/portlligat; mid-Feb–mid-June and mid-Sept–Dec Tue–Sun 10.30am–6pm, mid-June–mid-Sept daily 9.30am–9pm; booking essential; charge). Dalí and Gala lived for many years in this house, in fact a collection of fishermen's cottages.

Set in a garden of gnarled olive trees (where a restored workshop features a new exhibition), the house offers insight into the Dalís' domestic life.

The swimming pool area is an example of Dalían kitsch: modelled on a pool at the Moorish Alhambra in Granada, it is embellished with a statue of Diana the Huntress, Michelin men and Pirelli tyres.

If it is time for lunch, **Hotel Port Lligat**, see ②, is just across the road.

PÚBOL

To continue the tour (by car only), head back in the direction of Figueres until you see signs for the C31 south to Girona. Continue on this road up to the C252, towards Púbol.

Castell Gala-Dalí

The highlight in Púbol is the **Castell Gala-Dalí** ❸ (Plaça Gala-Dalí; www.salvador-dali.org/museus/pubol; mid-June–mid-Sept daily 10am–8pm, mid-Mar–mid-June, mid-Sept–Oct Tue–Sun 10.30am–6pm, Nov–Dec Tue–Sat 10am–5pm; charge). Dalí restored this Gothic-Renaissance castle for Gala in 1970. He painted frescoes in the interior and built the crypt where Gala is buried.

DIRECTORY

Hand-picked hotels and restaurants to suit all budgets and tastes, organised by area, plus select nightlife listings, an alphabetical listing of practical information, a language guide and an overview of the best books and films to give you a flavour of the city.

ACCOMMODATION

Millions of people visit Barcelona each year and there is no shortage of accommodation to suit all tastes and budgets. The 1992 Olympics left a legacy that transformed the hotel scene beyond recognition: old palaces were restored and turned into hotels, sparkling high-rises line the waterfront and run-down establishments have been given a new lease of life. Prices range from very expensive to good-value budget accommodation; and self-catering apartments are becoming very popular.

Renting a flat rather than staying in a hotel is becoming ever more popular, especially with families, as they offer the opportunity to self-cater, enabling shopping in the market and cutting holiday costs. Browse websites www.flatsbydays.com or www.oh-barcelona.com, which have a range of flats on their books. For a more luxurious option, try www.cru2001.com.

Fortunately for the Northern European and North American tourists who take their holidays in mid-summer, July and August are not considered peak times in hotel terms; September and October are in fact the peak months, when rooms will be more expensive and harder to find.

Sea views

There are several additional hotels along the rejuvenated waterfront near Diagonal Mar where high standard accommodation can be found at a reasonable price. As they are a taxi or metro ride from the centre, they are less popular, but the advantage of sea views and more peaceful nights is well worth considering.

La Rambla

1898
La Rambla 109; tel: 93 552 95 52; www.hotel1898.com; €€€€
This building was the headquarters of the Philippines Tobacco company until 1898 when the Philippines gained independence from Spain. Now it is a swish hotel with sound-proofed rooms and an upmarket colonial elegance.

Bagués
La Rambla, 105; tel: 93 343 50 00; www.derbyhotels.com; €€€
The jewel in the Derby Hotels crown is, fittingly, a former jewellery shop in prime position on La Rambla, right next to La Boqueria market. It's all about attention

> Price guide for a double room for one night with breakfast:
> €€€€ = over 200 euros
> €€€ = 140–200 euros
> €€ = 70–140 euros
> € = below 70 euros

1898 has a heated rooftop pool, open all year round

to detail and elegant finishes using gold leaf and ebony. Even the swimming pool on the roof is slimline.

Barcelona House

Carrer del Escudellers, 19; tel: 93343 71 67; www.hotel-barcelonahouse.com; €€

Recently renovated in a funky, colourful style and located close to the nightlife in the Plaça Reial in a slightly edgy street, this good-value hotel is ideal for a youngish crowd. Rooms have basic comforts plus en-suite bathrooms.

Catalunya Plaza

Plaça de Catalunya, 7; tel: 93 317 71 71; www.h10hotels.com; €€€

Recently refurbished into a plush boutique hotel with elaborate decoration that brings out the best of the original 19th-century features. The chill-out garden is an oasis in this vibrant, strategic square. It's hard to get more central than this.

Citadines Barcelona-Ramblas

La Rambla 122; tel: 93 270 11 11; www.citadines.com; €€€

An excellent-value apartment-hotel with a pleasant breakfast buffet bar and rooftop views. Buy food at the nearby Boqueria market.

Continental

La Rambla 138; tel: 93 301 25 70; www.hotelcontinental.com; €€

In a prime position near the top of La Rambla, this is an historic hotel with individual character. Swirling carpets and floral decor can be forgiven when you can sit on a balcony watching the world go by – and at a reasonable price. Ask for a room at the front.

D.O. Plaça Reial

Plaça Reial, 1; tel: 93 481 36 66; www.hoteldoreial.es; €€€€

The city's first gastronomic boutique hotel is in a handsome building, with smart interior decor, overlooking this legendary square. Enjoy the contemporary Catalan cuisine of Pere Moreno in La Cuina restaurant or on the exclusive rooftop, where there is also a small plunge pool.

Husa Internacional

La Rambla 78–80 ; tel: 93 302 25 66; www.husa.es.es; €€€

While retaining its original character outside, the hotel has been completely refurbished within to offer a fresh new minimalist image. Some rooms have a private balcony, and all windows are soundproofed. The rooftop chill-out terrace offers possibly one of the best views over the historic city.

Husa Oriente

La Rambla 45; tel: 93 302 25 58; www.hotelhusaoriente.com; €€€

Once an old favourite, after refurbishment it has recovered some of its former glory, including the splendid ballroom, but lost some of its personality.

Double room at the Racó del Pi

Kabul
Plaça Reial 17; tel: 93 318 51 90;
www.kabul.es; €
Long-established youth hostel in a privileged position on this grand square just off La Rambla. Rooms extend to dormitories for up to 20 guests. Known for its party atmosphere.

Onix Liceo
Nou de la Rambla, 36; tel: 93 481 64 41;
www.onixliceohotel.com; €€€
This elegant eco-friendly hotel, just off the lower part of La Rambla near the Palau Güell, has a minimalist style showing off the handsome decorative details of the grand building it occupies. The inner patio, with a sleek pool, is a haven away from the throngs in the street.

Barri Gòtic

Call
Carrer de l'Arc de Sant Ramon del Call 4;
tel: 93 302 11 23; www.hotelcall.es; €
A clean, small, air-conditioned 1-star hotel in the shady lanes of the Barri Gòtic. No bar or restaurant but everything you want is on your doorstep.

Catalonia Portal de l'Angel
Avinguda del Portal de l'Àngel 17; tel: 93 318 41 41; www.hoteles-catalonia.com; €€€
Housed in a stylish old building on one of Barcelona's busiest pedestrian shopping streets. Rooms are large and tastefully furnished, and there is a very nice garden patio with a pool.

Colón
Avinguda Catedral, 7; tel: 93 301 14 04;
www.colonhotelbarcelona.com; €€€
A legendary hotel overlooking the cathedral. The classically decorated bedrooms seem more English than Spanish. To feel really privileged, request a top-floor room with a private terrace so you're eye-to-eye with the spires.

Gótico
Carrer de Jaume I 14; tel: 93 315 22 11;
www.hotelgotico.com; €€€
In one of the Barri Gòtic's main streets, this soundproofed hotel has 81 rooms, some with a terrace, and a sundeck. Thoroughly modern and tasteful, it is handy, light and clean.

Gran Hotel Barcino
Carrer de Jaume I 6; tel: 93 302 20 12;
www.hotelbarcino.com; €€
In the heart of the Barri Gòtic, this modern hotel is chic and very well designed. The large, airy lobby does, however, overshadow the rooms.

El Jardí
Plaça de Sant Josep Oriol 1; tel: 93 301 59 00; www.eljardi-barcelona.com; €€
Small hotel overlooking two of the prettiest plazas in Barcelona. The rooms are a bargain, although a plaza view costs a little more. Recently renovated and very popular so book well ahead.

Hostal Lausanne
Portal de l'Àngel, 24,1°,1ª; tel: 93 302

Reception, Racó del Pi

Palatial exterior, Racó del Pi

11 39; www.hostallausanne.es;
€€
In a dream location for shoppers in this pedestrian street between Plaça de Catalunya and the cathedral, this homely place has retained some of the 19th-century elegance of the building where it is located.

Levante
Baixada de Sant Miquel 2; tel: 93 317 95 65; www.hostallevante.com; €
Basic accommodation with friendly atmosphere. Prides itself on the tale that the young Picasso was a frequent visitor in its former life as a house of ill repute. Just off Carrer d'Avinyó, one of the trendiest streets in the area.

Mercer
Carrer dels Lledó, 7; tel: 93 310 74 80; www.mercerbarcelona.com; €€€€
Feel the multi-layered history of the city in this stunning new boutique hotel in a former Gothic palace located on part of the Roman wall. Feast on gourmet delicacies, relaxed tapas and uplifting cocktails or chill in the rooftop pool between two Roman watchtowers.

Neri
Carrer de Sant Sever 5; tel: 93 304 06 55; www.hotelneri.com; €€€€
Elegant boutique hotel in a 17th-century palace overlooking one of the most atmospheric squares, near the cathedral. Roof terrace has views over medieval spires. Only 22 rooms.

Nouvel Hotel
Carrer de Santa Ana 18–20; tel: 93 301 82 74; www.hotelnouvel.com; €€€
On a pedestrianised street between La Rambla and Portal d'Àngel, this small hotel has a wonderful Modernista lobby and dining room. Rooms are plainer, but spacious and well equipped.

Ohla
Via Laietana 49; tel: 93 341 50 50; www.ohlahotel.com; €€€€
Opened in 2011, this 5-star hotel occupies a former department store renovated under the guidance of Catalan designer Frederic Amat. Behind its neoclassical facade are monochrome chic interiors, conference facilities, a wellness centre and the Sauc Michelin-starred restaurant. The crowning glory is a rooftop deck with glass-sided pool.

Racó del Pi
Carrer Pi 7; tel: 93 342 61 90; www.hotel h10racodelpi.com; €€€
In the very heart of the Barri Gòtic, around the corner from the Plaça del Pi, this small hotel sits within an old palace. There are only 37 rooms so it tends to get booked up early.

Sant Pere, La Ribera and El Born

Banys Orientals
Carrer de l'Argenteria 37; tel: 93 268 84 60; www.hotelbanysorientals.com; €€

Contemporary design at the Park Hotel

One of the city's best options, with impeccable slick interiors and stylish details, and in the best spot for shopping, wining and dining. There are also separate apartments. On the ground floor is the excellent restaurant Senyor Parellada (see page 114). Unbeatable value, so book well in advance.

chic&basic Born

Carrer de la Princesa 50; tel: 93 295 46 52; www.chicandbasic.com; €€–€€€

Rather more chic than basic, this stylish, ultra-modern hotel is situated in a handsome 19th-century building, well located between the Parc de la Ciutadella and the trendy El Born area. Surprisingly good value.

K&K Hotel Picasso

Passeig de Picasso, 26–30; tel: 93 547 86 00; www.kkhotels.com/en/hotels/barcelona; €€€€

A new business-like hotel made appealing because of its position overlooking the Parc de la Ciutadella, especially from a lounger by the rooftop pool.

Park Hotel

Avinguda del Marquès de l'Argentera 11; tel: 93 319 60 00; www.parkhotelbarcelona. com; €€€

A gem of 1950s architecture, quite rare in Barcelona, opposite the Estació de França, and near the Parc de la Ciutadella. On the edge of the Born district, which is awash with cafés, restaurants and bars and within walking distance of Barceloneta beach.

Pensió 2000

Carrer Sant Pere Més Alt 6, 1st floor; tel: 93 310 74 66; www.pensio2000.com; €€

An elegant marble staircase leads to this friendly family-run guesthouse, which is a cut above the average *pension* and right opposite the Palau de la Música Catalana. Great value.

Pension Ciudadela

Carrer del Comerç, 33, 1st floor; tel: 93 319 62 03; www.pension-ciudadela.com; €

Opposite the Estació de França, this humble guesthouse has decent rooms at a very reasonable price, and is within staggering distance of El Born nightlife.

El Raval

Casa Camper

Carrer d'Elisabets 11; tel: 93 342 62 80; www.casacamper.com; €€€

The first hotel to be opened by the sunny Mallorcan shoemakers is as chic as you might expect; 25 rooms designed by Fernando Amat and Jordi Tió in an imposing 19th-century building.

chic&basic Ramblas

Passatge Gutenberg, 7; tel: 93 302 71 11; www.chicandbasic.com; €€€

The creativity of this ingenious small Catalan chain is irrepressible. Their latest venture has a 1960s theme, in

Stylish restaurant at the Park Hotel

keeping with its funky building. The comfortable rooms and communal areas are fun and colourful as well as being excellent value.

España

Carrer de Sant Pau 11; tel: 93 550 00 00; www.hotelespanya.com; €€€

Just off the lower part of La Rambla, the España retains a flavour of bygone days. The beautiful public rooms were designed by the Modernista architect Domènech i Montaner. The recently refurbished guest rooms perfectly blend timeless style with the classicism of the 19th-century building.

Grau

Carrer Ramelleres 27; tel: 93 301 81 35; www.hostalgrau.com; €€

Book early for this popular, well-kept *pension*, which is in a good position for shopping and visiting both the Eixample and Old Town. Excellent breakfasts in the adjoining bar.

Inglaterra

Carrer de Pelai 14; tel: 93 505 11 00; www.hotel-inglaterra.com; €€€

A contemporary hotel set behind a handsome old facade, and equally well located for the bohemian Raval or the elegant Eixample. Stands out from the crowd in its price range. The lovely rooftop terrace offers amazing views.

Mesón de Castilla

Carrer de Valldonzella, 5; tel: 93 318 21 82; www.mesoncastilla.com; €€€

The furniture is old-fashioned and rustic in style and the place is a bit quirky, but at least it has individual character. Very good location near the CCCB, university and shops. The owners are friendly and helpful.

Peninsular

Carrer de Sant Pau 34; tel: 93 302 31 38; www.hotelpeninsular.net; €

In an old Augustian monastery, with rooms around a charming inner courtyard. Rooms are basic but good value for money, and staff are helpful and friendly.

Raval Rooms

Carrer Hospital 155, 1st floor; tel: 93 324 88 33; www.ravalrooms.com; €€

Almost nursery-school cheerful, this modern hotel in the city's old hospital street attracts young clued-up travellers. The hotel offers single and double rooms with a 'basic kit' of shower and toilet. Rooms are not large, but suites offer extra space. There's a terrace on the hotel roof for chilling out.

Sant Agustí

Plaça Sant Agustí, 3; tel: 93 318 16 58; www.hotelsa.com; €€€

The oldest hotel in Barcelona overlooks a peaceful square. Recently spruced up, it is well worth paying more for one of the luxury rooms located on the fourth floor.

Bird's-eye view of the W Barcelona

The waterfront

Arts
Passeig de la Marina 19–21; tel: 93 221
10 00: www.hotelartsbarcelona.com;
€€€€
A high-tech, ultra-deluxe high-rise, situated right by the beach in Vila Olímpica. Extremely efficient, decorated with sophisticated, understated taste. Large rooms, huge bathrooms and amazing views.

Barcelona Princess
Avinguda Diagonal 1; tel: 93 356 10 00;
www.hotelbarcelonaprincess.com; €€€€
On the cutting edge in all senses: designed by leading Catalan architect Oscar Tusquets, situated in the rejuvenated district of the Diagonal Mar, and offering all possible facilities. Prices are subject to radical cuts, so it is worth trying to bargain for the benefit of sleeping at this giddy height, with great views of sea and city.

Duquesa de Cardona
Passeig de Colom 12; tel: 93 268 90 90;
www.hduqesadecardona.com; €€€
A classically elegant hotel set in the long-overlooked, handsome buildings giving on to the original waterfront and the old harbour. The pool and terrace on the roof are a hidden treasure. Luxury at a moderate price.

Equity Point Sea
Plaça del Mar 4; tel: 93 224 70 75;
www.equity-point.com; €
An unbeatable position for a youth hostel, right on Barceloneta beach. This chain of youth hostels also has a branch in La Ribera (Point Gothic) and one up in Gràcia (Point Centric).

Front Marítim
Passeig de García Faria 69–71; tel: 93
303 44 40; www.hotelfrontmaritim.com;
€€–€€€
On the waterfront between the Vila Olímpica and Diagonal Mar. It is just a taxi ride away from the inner city buzz, but you wake up to sea views. Slick and comfortable.

Grand Marina
World Trade Centre, Moll de Barcelona, 1;
tel: 93 603 90 00; www.grandmarinahotel.com; €€€€
You feel as if you are aboard a luxurious cruise ship. Some of the bedrooms, with hydro-massage baths, jut out into the port, while those at the rear have a panoramic view of the city.

Hotel 54
Passeig Joan de Borbó, 54; tel: 93 225 00
54; www.hotel54barceloneta.es; €€€
A modern hotel in an extraordinary location in Barceloneta overlooking the port and city, so you can enjoy the sea, but still easily walk to the centre. The building was once the fishermen's headquarters.

Marina Folch
Carrer del Mar, 16, pral (1st floor); tel: 93

Luxury suite, W Barcelona   *Suite terrace, W Barcelona*

310 37 09; email:marinafolchbcn@hotmail.com; €€
This is a family-run gem with only 11 rooms, so book in advance. Request a room overlooking the busy waterfront for fun, or at the rear for a more peaceful night.

W Barcelona
Plaça de la Rosa del Vents, tel: 93 295 28 00; www.w-barcelona.com; €€€€
Rising 26 floors above the Mediterranean, and marking the entrance to Barcelona's harbour, is an avant-garde icon of the city's dynamic post-modern architecture. Shaped like a billowing sail, the long-awaited W Barcelona hotel, the work of Spanish architect Ricardo Bofill, opened in 2009.

The Eixample

Actual
Carrer del Rosselló 238; tel: 93 552 05 50; www.hotelactual.com; €€€
Situated on the same block as Gaudí's La Pedrera, this well-equipped, contemporary hotel offers minimalist decor in dark brown and white combined with a warm, personal atmosphere. It is sought after, so book well in advance.

Axel
Carrer d'Aribau, 33; tel: 93 323 93 93; www.axelhotels.com/barcelona; €€€
This hetero-friendly gay hotel located in the 'Gaixample' is one of the most beautiful in the city. Behind the *modern-ista* facade of stained-glass balconies there are stylish rooms and an urban spa. Every indulgence.

Balmes Hotel
Carrer de Mallorca 216; tel: 93 451 19 14; www.derbyhotels.com; €€€
The Balmes promises 'the advantages of the countryside in the heart of the city', and has an attractive leafy garden and a pool. Good location.

Casa Fuster
Passeig de Gràcia 132; tel: 93 255 30 00; www.hotelescenter.es; €€€€
Classified as a five-star 'Monument' hotel, Casa Fuster, built by Domènech i Montaner in 1908, has been restored to its Modernista splendour. Facilities include the Café Viennese, the Galaxó restaurant, a jacuzzi and gym, plus a roof terrace pool, from where there are gorgeous views. A member of the Leading Small Hotels of the World.

Hostal Cèntric
Carrer de Casanova, 13; tel: 93 426 75 73; www.hostalcentric.com; €€
New-generation guesthouse, fresh, clean, modern and recently renovated. Excellent value and within walking distance of the Old Town and the Eixample.

Circa 1905
Carrer de Provenza 286; tel: 93 505 69 60; www.circa1905.com; €€€
This well-kept secret on the first floor of a Modernista building offers a privileged

location from which to explore Catalan Modernism. Just nine renovated rooms, some of which have balconies.

Condes de Barcelona
Passeig de Gràcia 75; tel: 93 445 00 00; www.condesdebarcelona.com; €€€€
Contemporary elegance in two Modernista buildings facing each other in the Quadrat d'Or area of the Eixample. The two Michelin-starred Lasarte restaurant is under the watchful eye of celebrated Basque chef Martìn Berasategui. There is a roof terrace with a mini pool.

Constanza
Carrer del Bruc 33; tel: 93 270 19 10; www.hotelconstanza.com; €€
Modern, efficient boutique hotel that should appeal to those with a funky youthful outlook. The rooms are not huge, but some have terraces.

Girona
Carrer de Girona 24, 1st floor; tel: 93 265 02 59; www.hostalgirona.com; €
A grand stone staircase rises from the elegant patio of this Modernista building designed by Idelfons Cerdà and situated in the area known as the Quadrat d'Or. The *hostal* is a good-value option in a very central location, with a warm, friendly reception from the Berlanga family.

Gran Hotel Havana Silken
Gran Vía de les Corts Catalanes 647; tel: 93 341 70 00; www.hoteles-silken.com; €€€
Classic and sophisticated style runs through this 1872 mansion. Barcelona's signature design elements are displayed in all the bedrooms, and on the panoramic roof terrace with a pool.

Granvía
Gran Vía de les Corts Catalanes 642; tel: 93 318 19 00; www.hotelgranvia.com; €€€
Housed in a neoclassical building that was constructed as a bourgeois palace, today the Granvia's rooms feature original 19th-century furnishings that ooze elegance and distinction. Very close to the Plaça de Catalunya and Passeig de Gràcia.

Indigo
Gran Vía de les Corts Catalanes, 629; tel: 93 165 13 81; www.indigobarcelona.com; €€€
The boutique branch of InterContinental has just opened this bright, cheerful hotel in an enviable location, just off Passeig de Gràcia. Handsome building, with a contemporary interior and a huge terrace with a pool.

Murmuri
Rambla de Catalunya, 104; tel: 93 492 22 44; www.murmuri.com €€€
The award-winning modern elegance of this boutique hotel fits in perfectly with the sophisticated surroundings of the upper part of Rambla de Catalunya

Reception at the achingly trendy Omm

and carries on through its apartments, housed in an adjacent building. This is high-end living.

Omm

Carrer del Rosselló 265; tel: 93 445 40 00; www.hotelomm.es; €€€€
Just off Passeig de Gràcia, this award-winning designer hotel is part of the seriously cool Tragaluz group. The rooms are stylish and well lit, and the rooftop pool is stunning, with views of Gaudí's La Pedrera. The in-house club is reckoned one of the best places to be on Barcelona's night scene.

Paseo de Gracia

Passeig de Gràcia 102; tel: 93 215 06 03; www.hotelpaseodegracia.es; €€
Another vestige from the past, with some original fittings. In the same block as La Pedrera, it is in a prime location and good value for money in this expensive area.

Praktik Rambla

Rambla Catalunya, 27; tel: 93 343 66 90; www.hotelpraktikrambla.com; €€
An amazingly stylish hotel, making the most of the building's *modernista* features but mixed with fresh, clean design and creative ideas. Has an attractive terrace in a typical Eixample interior patio. Great location between Old Town and Eixample.

The 5 Rooms

Carrer de Pau Claris 72, 1st floor; tel: 93 342 78 80; www.thefiverooms.com; €€
As the name suggests, just five guest rooms make up this romantic bed-and-breakfast place, tucked away in the heart of the Eixample neighbourhood. Stylish, modern and thoughtfully decorated, it bills itself as a 'cocooning' concept to make you feel at home.

Montjuïc

Mambo Tango Hostal

Carrer del Poeta Cabanyes, 23; tel: 93 442 51 64; www.hostelmambotango.com; €
Private rooms are available but the fun begins in the dorms. Lively, good-value hostel with very friendly staff in a great position amid the nightlife of Poble Sec.

Milleni

Ronda Sant Pau, 14; tel: 93 441 41 77; www.hotel-millennibarcelona.com; €€€
This medium-sized modernised hotel lies on the edge of the Old Town so is within easy reach of the historical treasures, Montjuïc and the trade fair site. Good deals for family rooms.

Hotel Miramar

Plaça Carlos Ibáñez; tel: 93 281 16 00; www.hotelmiramarbarcelona.es; €€€€
In prime position on the hilltop, these former TV studios have been transformed by local star architect Tusqets into a luxury hotel offering full-on indulgence. For the best views, ask for a room overlooking the port.

RESTAURANTS

Barcelona offers the world on a plate, with cuisines from around the globe. It is, however, Catalan food that catches the imagination, with an emphasis on first-class seasonal and fresh produce, used from Michelin-starred establishments to humble tapas bars. Choose from the elegant surroundings of five-star hotels, seafood restaurants with a beach view, sleek modern bistros and tiny tapas bars, or explore the backstreets for traditional family-run restaurants, where time has stood still.

La Rambla

Amaya
La Rambla 20–4; tel: 93 302 10 37; www.restauranteamaya.com; daily 1–4pm, 7–11.30pm; €€€
A Basque restaurant run by the fourth generation of the Torralba family. The cosy dining room stays true to its original style and there is a lovely terrace.

Attic
La Rambla, 120; tel: 93 302 48 66; daily

> Price guide for a three-course à la carte dinner for one with a bottle of house wine:
> €€€€ = over 60 euros
> €€€ = 40–60 euros
> €€= 25–40 euros
> € = below 25 euros

1–4.30pm, 6.30pm–12.30am; €€
Part of a chain that produces authentic Spanish cuisine on a large scale, but does so effectively, creating a good ambience. Popular with tourists. The tables overlooking La Rambla provide an irresistible floor show and the roof terrace is perfect.

Bar Lobo
Carrer del Pintor Fortuny, 3; tel: 93 481 53 46; www.grupotragaluz.com/restaurantes/bar-lobo; daily 9am–midnight (Sat–Sun until 2.30am); €€
The hippest member of the Tragaluz empire attracts a cool crowd with its stylish interior, lounging terrace in a busy pedestrian street, and combination of light Mediterranean and Japanese dishes. Open late for drinks at weekends.

Egipte
La Rambla 79; tel: 93 317 95 45; www.egipte-ramblas.com; daily noon–1am; €
A lively, popular place just near the Boqueria. Once a small eatery within the market itself, Egipte is now spread over several floridly decorated floors.

Fresc Co
Carrer del Carme 16; tel: 93 318 75 16; daily 12.45pm–1am; €
Just past the church of Betlem, this is one in a chain of self-service restau-

Super-fresh fish

rants offering all you can eat for under €10.

Kiosko Universal
Mercat Sant Josep (La Boqueria), Parada 691; tel: 93 317 82 86; Mon–Sat 8am–5pm; €€
Pull up a stool at the bar amid the market's stallholders and eat the freshest of produce, cooked before your eyes. Try their specials, octopus and shellfish.

Luzia
Carrer del Pintor Fortuny, 1; tel: 93 342 96 28; www.grupotragaluz.com/en/restaurants/luzia; daily 8.30am–midnight; €€ (set menu L €)
Mediterranean to the gills, this is a great place to have a healthy snack at any time of day, from creative sandwiches to pizzas cooked in a wood-fired oven. Main courses include vegetarian-friendly dishes.

Les Quinze Nits
Plaça Reial 6; tel: 93 317 30 75; daily 12.30–11.30pm; €€
This popular restaurant, serving Mediterranean cuisine, is well situated in the Plaça Reial. It is a good spot for a meal at any time, but the inexpensive set-lunch menu is particularly good value.

Barri Gòtic

Agut
Carrer d'en Gignàs 16; tel: 93 315 17 09; www.restaurantagut.com; Tue–Sat 1–4pm, 8.30–11.30pm, Sun 1.30–4pm; €€

This historic restaurant is hidden down a small street. Relaxed, with a bohemian feel, it has plenty of Catalan flavour and lots of specials. The excellent huge rice dishes are meant to be shared.

L'Antic Bocoi del Gòtic
Baixada de Viladecols, 3; tel: 93 310 50 67; www.bocoi.net; Mon–Sat 7.30pm–midnight; €
Inspiring, delicious Catalan specialities like the *coques* (a kind of pizza with interesting toppings), plus imaginative salads. The warm and characterful interior incorporates part of the Roman city wall.

ATN
Carrer de la Canuda 6; tel: 93 318 52 38; www.atnrestaurant.cat; Mon 10am–6.30pm, Tue–Sat 10.30am–12.30am; €€
The restaurant in the Ateneu Barcelonès cultural centre, beside Plaça de la Vila de Madrid, serves hearty Catalan farmyard favourites including duck, goose and rabbit.

Bosco
Carrer dels Capellans, 9; tel: 93 412 13 70; Tue–Sat 1pm–5pm, 8–11.30pm, Mon 1–5pm; €€
Hidden from the shopping crowds of Portal de l'Angel is this peaceful restaurant with a terrace on the quiet square, where there is a play area for kids. Fresh fish and seasonal vegetables from La Boqueria are on the good-value lunchtime set menu.

Chocolate and churros

La Brasserie du Gothique

Hotel Catalonia Catedral, Carrer dels Arcs; tel: 93 318 70 66; www.brasserie-gothique. com; daily 1–4pm, 8–11pm; €€

If you are here at lunch time this French hotel restaurant is a calm retreat from the busy tourist area. Choose from a menu that includes duck cannelloni, scallops and fondues. Seating inside and out.

Can Culleretes

Carrer d'en Quintana 5; tel: 93 317 30 22; www.culleretes.com; Tue–Sat 1.30–4pm, 9–11pm, Sun 1.30–4pm, closed mid-July to mid-Aug; €

Barcelona's oldest restaurant has served traditional Catalan food since 1786. It is cosy and informal, and has tasty classics including *espinacas à la catalana* (spinach with pine nuts and raisins).

Los Caracoles

Carrer d'Escudellers 14; tel: 93 301 20 41; www.loscaracoles.es; daily 1pm–midnight; €€€

'The Snails' is famous for the chicken on spits outside. It has been around since 1835. Touristy but fun, and you can get fish, game, chicken or lamb, in addition to the speciality caracoles.

La Fonda

Carrer dels Escudellers, 10; tel: 93 301 75 15; www.lafonda-restaurant.com; daily 1–11.30pm; € (set menu Mon–Sat D €)

The popularity of this restaurant, part of the expanding Quinze Nits family, comes from its appealing decor and reasonably priced market-fresh food. Keep an eye on your belongings as you stand in the inevitable queue.

Matsuri

Plaça Regomir, 1; tel: 93 268 15 35; www.matsuri-restaurante.com; daily 8pm–midnight; €€

Filling a gap in the market, this good-looking restaurant specialises in Southeast Asian food, which is given a personal interpretation by its creative chef.

El Portalon

Carrer de Banys Nous 20; tel: 93 302 11 87; www.elportalonbcn.com; Mon–Sat 9am–midnight; €

This is a typical *bodega* with wine barrels and tapas. Offers good value and authentic ambience.

Reial Cercle Artístic

Carrer dels Arcs 5; tel: 93 301 59 37; www.ovellanegra.com; Tue–Sat 1–4pm, 8pm–midnight; € (lunch), €€ (dinner)

Treat yourself to a light lunch of cheese, pâté or salad on the terrace of this impressive palace or come back later for a more substantial dinner.

Shunka

Carrer del Sagristans 5; tel: 93 412 49 91; daily 1.30–3.30pm, 8.30–11.30pm; €€€

Hidden behind the cathedral is one of the best Japanese restaurants in the city. Love and wisdom goes into the

Fishy tapas   *Flan (flam in Catalan) is ubiquitous*

preparation of top-quality specialities right in front of your eyes.

Sant Pere, La Ribera, El Born and Ciutadella

Bascula
Carrer dels Flassaders, 30 bis; tel: 93-319 9866; Wed–Sun 1–11.30pm; €
A new kind of restaurant, run as a co-operative by people from many different countries, in a former chocolate factory in the labyrinth of streets behind the Picasso Museum. Delicious snacks and wholesome meals using organic produce, mostly vegetarian.

Cal Pep
Plaça de les Olles 8; tel: 93 310 79 61; www.calpep.com; Tue–Fri 1–3.45pm, 7.30–11.30pm, Mon 7.30–11.30pm, Sat 1–3.45pm; €€€
A boisterous bar in El Born that does some of the best seafood in Barcelona. Join the cava-sipping queue for a seat at the counter where you can watch delectable little dishes being prepared.

Comerç 24
Carrer del Comerç, 24; tel: 93 319 21 02; www.carlesabellan.es; Tue–Sat 1.30–3.30pm, 8.30–11pm . €€€€
One of the leading lights in new-wave Catalan cooking, chef Carles Abellán, inspired by several years working in the laboratory-kitchen of El Bullí, has several restaurants in the city. This designer-smart but relaxed space was the first. Choose between two tasting menus, the *Festival de Tapas* or the *Gran Festival* – both are a trip for the taste buds.

Cuines de Santa Caterina
Avinguda de Francesc Cambó 20; tel: 93 268 99 18; daily 1–4pm, 8–11.30pm; €€
Sit at the bar for a drink and tapas or, for a heartier meal, at one of the tables in this modern, bright emporium within the Santa Caterina market. Market-fresh food is used in the Mediterranean, Oriental and vegetarian dishes.

Espai Sucre
Carrer de la Princesa 53; tel: 93 268 16 30; www.espaisucre.com; Mon–Thu 9–11.30pm, Fri–Sat first sitting 8.30pm, second 10.30pm; €€€
Desserts only are served at this inventive restaurant. However, they include 'salads', 'soups' and other concoctions never found in a cake shop – or anywhere else. Excellent dessert wines accompany the three- to five-course meals.

Passadis de Pep
Plaça de Palau 2; tel: 93 310 10 21; www.passadis.com; Mon–Sat 1.15–3.45pm, 8.30–11.30pm; €€€€
A rustic restaurant with no menu – they just keep bringing you the dishes – which presents skilfully cooked seafood using the freshest ingredients; a culinary experience for fish lovers.

Senyor Parellada

Pla de la Garsa

Carrer dels Assaonadors, 13; tel: 93 315 24 13; www.pladelagarsa.com; daily 8pm–midnight; €€

This tastefully restored medieval stable with attractive decor is a peaceful option for an evening meal. Enjoy Catalan specialities, especially their range of cheeses, pâtés and *embotits* (cured sausages, ham and typical pork products).

Santa Maria

Carrer del Comerç 17; tel: 93 315 12 27; www.santarestaurant.wordpress.com; Tue–Thu noon–11pm, Fri–Sat noon–midnight; €€

Chef Paco Guzman promotes the rare idea of gourmet food at manageable prices, with his dainty little dishes of Mediterranean and Oriental extraction.

Senyor Parellada

Carrer de l'Argentería 37; tel: 93 310 50 94; www.senyorparellada.com; daily 1–4pm, 8.30pm–midnight; €€€

An attractive, popular spot owned and run by the family that owns the adjoining Banys Orientals hotel. The purely Catalan menu is based on unpretentious home-made dishes.

7 Portes

Passeig d'Isabel II; tel: 93 319 30 33; www.7portes.com; daily 1pm–1am; €€

Sympathetically restored, recapturing the original atmosphere, this 160-year-old classic specialises in rice dishes, one for each day of the week.

Va de Vi

Carrer de Banys Vells 16; tel: 93 319 29 00; Tue–Wed 6pm–1am, Thu 6pm–2am, Fri–Sat 6pm–3am; €€

Cavernous old wine bar with a modern designer touch. Great place to try the best of Spain's wines and local artisanal produce.

La Vinya del Senyor

Plaça de Santa Maria 5; tel: 93 310 33 79; Tue–Thu and Sun noon–1am, Fri–Sat noon–2am; €€€

The Lord's Vineyard is a classic wine bar in a great spot on the square. Excellent tapas and an incredibly wide selection of wines.

El Xampanyet

Carrer de Montcada 22; tel: 93 319 70 03; daily noon–4pm, 6.30–11.30pm, closed Aug; €€

Wash down the house speciality, anchovies, with cava, served in wide-brimmed glasses. Tiny bar with a big atmosphere.

El Raval

L'Antic Forn

Carrer del Pintor Fortuny 28; tel: 93 412 02 86; www.lanticforn.com; Mon–Sat 9am–5pm, 8pm–midnight; €

The 'Old Bakery' is an informal place spread over different spaces, which enjoys a good reputation for Catalan cuisine that won't disappoint you, at affordable prices.

La Vinya del Senyor

Ca L'Isidre

Carrer de les Flors 12; tel: 93 441 11 39;
www.calisidre.com; Mon–Sat 1.30–4pm,
8.30–11pm; €€€ (set lunch Mon–Fri €€)
A family-owned restaurant producing
fine traditional cuisine with a contemporary twist, and sumptuous desserts.
Excellent service.

Can Lluís

Carrer de la Cera, 49; tel: 93-441 1187;
www.restaurantcanlluis.cat;
Mon–Sat 1.30–4pm, 8.30–11.30pm;
€€
Can Lluís is the kind of genuine Catalan restaurant you would hope to find
in a small village, so it's a pleasant sur-
prise to encounter it in the heart of the
city. Delicious food, like *favetes minis
amb xipironets* (tender broad beans
with baby squid) or *suquet* (a rich fish
stew) is served amid noise and bustle,
and no pretensions. Excellent value
lunchtime menu.

Casa Leopoldo

Carrer de Sant Rafael 24; tel: 93 441 69
42; www.casaleopoldo.com; Tue–Sat
1.30–3.30pm, 8.30–10.30pm, Sun
1.30–3.30pm; €€€
Tucked away in the Barri Xino, this place
serves excellent Catalan stews.

Dos Palillos

Carrer d'Elisabets 9; 93 304 05
13; www.dospalillos.com; Thu–Sat
1.30–3.30pm, 7.30–11.30pm, Tue–Wed
7.30–11.30pm; €€

This is a smart, trendy place with the
unusual concept of a choice of Asian
food or Spanish tapas, presented and
cooked to a high standard. Note that
lunch is only served from Thursday to
Saturday.

Dos Trece

Carrer del Carme, 40; tel: 93 301 73 06;
www.dostrece.net; daily 10am–midnight; €
Fashionable place with a laid-back atti-
tude and good atmosphere. Unconven-
tional, tasty dishes show the influence
of the owner's Mexican/LA background.
Serves good brunch at weekends.

En Ville

Carrer del Doctor Dou, 14; tel: 93 302 84
67; www.envillebarcelona.es; Tue–Sat 1–4,
8–11.30pm, Mon 1–4pm; €€ (set menu L
& D €)
Creative Catalan cooking with a French
edge in charming, spacious surroundings. Marble tables, palms and gentle
live music (Tue and Wed) complete the
picture. Good value.

Elisabets

Carrer d'Elisabets 2; tel: 93 317 58 26;
Mon–Sat 7.30am–11pm; €
Bustling local bar popular for generous
home-made dishes and a good-value
set menu.

Maharaja

Rambla del Raval, 14 tel: 93 442 57 77;
www.maharajarestaurante.com; daily
noon–1am; €

Delicate tapas

The ultimate in Spanish-Indian crossover has to be the biryani paella served here on an open-air terrace in the middle of this new rambla. The more traditional Indian dishes are good, too, and there are plenty of vegetarian options.

La Reina del Raval

Rambla del Raval 5; tel: 93 443 36 55; daily 1.30–3.30pm, 8.30–11pm; €€€
With big windows looking onto the Rambla, this bright modern space has a young clientele and features an eclectic menu with market ingredients. There is a gourmet menu, an à la carte and a lunch-time set menu, plus tapas.

Sesamo

Carrer de Sant Antoni Abat 52; tel: 93 441 64 11; Tue–Sun 8am–midnight; €
Close to Sant Antoni market, this inviting vegetarian place sells good spicy dishes. The tasting menu is a delight.

Suculent

Rambla del Raval, 43; tel: 93 443 65 79; www.suculent.com; Tue–Sat 12.30pm–1am, Sun lunch only; €€
A great addition to the area with superstar chef Carles Abellan in the wings, though young chef Antonio Romero produces traditional Catalan dishes with a contemporary edge masterfully. Try their take-away fried potatoes if nothing else.

The Waterfront

Agua

Passeig Marítim 30; tel: 93 225 12 72; www.grupotragaluz.com; Mon–Fri 1–3.45pm, 8–11.30pm Sat–Sun 1–4.30pm, 8pm–12.30am; €€
Almost on the beach, with tables indoors and out, the modern, attractive Agua gets very busy, especially at lunch time, so booking is essential. Well-prepared fish and seafood, rice dishes, and imaginative vegetarian dishes.

Barceloneta

Carrer de l'Escar 22; tel 93 221 21 11; www.restaurantbarceloneta.com; daily 1pm–1am; €€€
The outdoor terrace, jutting out above the fishing boats and smooth yachts of Port Vell, makes this one of the most perfect places to eat seafood dishes.

Bestial

Carrer de Ramon Trias i Fargas 2–4; tel: 93 224 04 07; www.grupotragaluz.com; Mon–Thu 1–3.45pm, Fri 1–3.45pm, 8pm–12.30am, Sat 1–4.30pm, 8pm–12.30am, Sun 1–4.30pm, 8–11.30pm; €€
A trendy place with a multi-level beachside terrace. Minimal decor and fine Italian-inspired rice and pasta.

Can Solé

Carrer de Sant Carles, 4; tel: 93 221 50 12; www.restaurantcansole.com; Tue–Sat 1–4pm, 8–11pm; Sun 1–4pm. €€€
In the heart of Barceloneta, literally and metaphorically, and a favourite with locals and Barcelona celebrities, Can Solé has been cooking great seafood and fish since 1903.

Can Majó

Almirall Aixada, 23; tel: 93 221 54 55; www.canmajo.es, Tue–Sat 1–4pm 8–11.30pm, Sun 1–4pm; €€€

This is one of the best and longest established of the Barceloneta seafood restaurants, where it's worth paying a bit extra to be sure of a good paella. Pretty decor indoors, but it also has a terrace on the pavement within sight of the sea.

Carballeira

Carrer de la Reina Cristina, 3; tel: 93 310 10 06; http://carballeira.com; Tue–Sat 1pm–midnight, Sun lunch only. €€€€

Excellent Galician fish and seafood dishes in an old-style restaurant. At lunchtime try a simple *tapa* of *arròs a la banda* (delicious rice cooked in fish stock) at the bar. Accompany it with a glass of Ribeira (Galician white wine), in particular, the cloudy variety, *turbio*.

Puda Can Manel

Passeig Joan de Borbó, 60–61; tel: 93 221 50 13; www.pudacanmanel.com; Tue–Sun 1–4.30pm, 8–11.30pm; €€

A good middle-range fish restaurant on this parade bursting with places that try to tempt you in. Here they don't have to bother. Get there early to find a place on the pretty terrace overlooking Port Vell.

Restaurant 1881 Per Sagardi

Museu d'Història de Catalunya, Palau de Mar; tel: 93; daily 10am–midnight; €€€

One reason for visiting the museum is to enjoy the restaurant on the top floor, with fine views over the port. Mediterranean food is served either in the elegant dining room or outside on the covered terrace.

Sal Café

Passeig Marítim; tel: 93 224 07 07; http://salcafe.com; Summer daily 1–3.30pm, 8.30–10.30pm, winter Sat–Sun only, depending on weather; €

Down on the Barceloneta beach near the climbing frame is this slick restaurant-cum-bar, the trendiest *xiringuito* around, serving exotic flavours. Handy for kids, with special menus and plenty of sand to play in.

Xiringuíto Escribà

Avinguda del Litoral Mar 42, Platja del Bogatell; tel: 93 221 07 29; www.xiringuito escriba.com; summer only Mon–Fri 1–4.30pm, 8–11pm, Sat–Sun 1–5pm, 8–11.30pm ; €€€

Lots of imaginative fish and rice dishes in this family-run establishment by the beach. The Escribà family is renowned for chocolates and pastries, so the puddings are guaranteed to be marvellous.

The Eixample

Alkimia

Carrer de la Indústria 79; tel: 93 207 61 15; www.alkimia.cat; Mon–Fri 1.30–3.30pm, 8.30–11pm; €€€€

Near the Sagrada Família, this is a shining example of the new talent in Cata-

lan cuisine. Renowned Michelin-starred chef Jordi Vilà is the alchemist, working wonders on ordinary Catalan dishes. Fast becoming one of Barcelona's leading restaurants.

Au Port de la Lune

Carrer de Pau Claris, 103; tel: 93 412 22 24; daily Mon–Fri 8am–11pm, Sat 10am–11pm, Sun 10am–7pm; €€

A poster of Serge Gainsbourg and a sign saying 'No coca cola, nor will there ever be' are the only clues to this neutral-looking café's provenance. However, the menu features steak tartare, *cassoulet* and herrings. Even the salad dressing tastes French. This is genuine 'cuisine'.

Casa Calvet

Carrer de Casp 48; tel: 93 412 40 12; www.casacalvet.es; Mon–Sat 1–3.30pm, 8.30–11pm; €€€€

On the first floor of one of Gaudí's first apartment buildings, Casa Calvet exudes elegant Modernista ambience. Tables are spaced well apart; some even occupy private booths, and the excellent Catalan menu is fairly priced.

El Caballito Blanco

Carrer de Mallorca 196; tel: 93 453 10 13; Tue–Sat 1.15–3.45pm, 8.45–10.45pm, Sun 1.15–3.45pm; €€€

An old-fashioned, popular place, using fresh seasonal ingredients. It is a relief to find places like this have escaped being redesigned and relaunched.

Fastvínic

Carrer de la Diputació, 251; tel: 93 487 32 41; www.fastvinic.com; Mon–Sat noon–midnight; €

The first restaurant in Catalonia to receive the LEED Gold certificate, this new-concept, good-looking, sustainable place serves unique sandwiches using locally sourced seasonal products based on Catalan dishes. Try a pig's trotter or river trout and fennel sandwich accompanied by one of 24 Catalan wines.

Gorría

Carrer de la Diputació 421; tel: 93 245 11 64; www.restaurantegorria.com; Mon–Sat 1–3.30pm, 9–11.30pm (closed Mon pm); €€€

Daily deliveries of fish from the north make this family-run place the perfect spot to eat quality Basque dishes.

Jaume de Provença

Carrer de Provença 88; tel: 93 430 00 29; www.jaumeprovenza.com; Tue–Sat 1–3.45pm, 9–11.15pm, Sun 1–3.45pm; €€€€

A small restaurant with a country flavour, near Sants station, named after innovative owner-chef Jaume Bargués. After nearly 30 years it is still considered to be a pioneer of creative cuisine and is correspondingly popular.

L'Olive

Carrer de Balmes 47; tel: 93 452 19 90; www.restaurantolive.com; Mon–Sat 1–4pm, 8.30–11.30pm, Sun 1–4pm; €€€

L'Olive has long been considered a fashionable place for classic Catalan dishes with an original touch, served in slick minimalist premises.

Moments

Hotel Mandarin Oriental, Passeig de Gràcia 38–48; tel: 93 151 87 81; www.mandarin oriental.com; Tue–Sat 1.30–3.30pm, 8.30–10.30pm; €€€€

Overseen by Carme Ruscalleda, the only female chef in the world to hold six Michelin stars, Moments stands out for its refreshing twist on Catalan dishes served amid stunning decor.

Tragaluz

Passatge de la Concepció 5; tel: 93 487 06 21; www.grupotragaluz.com; daily 1.30–4pm, 8.30pm–11.30pm; €€€€

An extensive, creative menu of Mediterranean food in a trendy restaurant where you can dine under a glass roof.

Montjüic

La Caseta del Migdia

Parc del Migdia; tel: 693-992760 (mobile); www.lacaseta.org; summer: Wed 9–midnight, Thu–Fri 8pm–midnight, Sat noon–2am, Sun noon–midnight; winter weekends lunch only, check for times; €

Alfresco rustic eating with an amazing view, hidden away in the pine trees near the castle. One of the few spots you can watch the sun set in the city. Try grilled sardines accompanied by rumba on summer nights, or take a picnic and buy drinks at the bar.

Fundació Miró bar restaurant

Fundació Miró, Avinguda de Miramar 1; tel: 93 329 07 68; Tue–Sat 1–3.45pm, Sun 1–2.30pm (bar only); €

Lovely restaurant with an outdoor courtyard and good staples such as pasta plus local dishes including an aromatic rabbit stew.

El Lliure

Teatre Lliure, Passeig Santa Madrona; tel: 93 237 12 43; Tue–Fri 1–4pm, and before and until two hours after performances; €€

This theatre restaurant has an innovative menu for indoor and outdoor meals.

Oleum

Palau Nacional; tel: 93 289 06 79; Tue–Sat 12.30–4pm, 7.30–11.30pm, Sun 12.30–4pm; €€

With panoramic views reflected in its mirrored ceiling, this smart restaurant serves Mediterranean food, using top-quality produce.

Tickets

Avinguda del Paral.lel 164; www.ticketsbar. es; Tue–Fri 7–11.30pm, Sat 1–3.30pm, 7–11.30pm, Sun 1–3.30pm (closed 3 weeks Aug); €€€€

Word has spread so fast about Ferran Adrià's spherical olives and hot cheese and ham airbags that you need to book months in advance via the website to get a look in at this high-end tapas bar with staff in circus garb. The Adrià Brothers' empire continues to spread, so watch out for new openings in this neighbourhood.

Busy Barcelona bar

NIGHTLIFE

To find out what's on pick up the free magazines *Barcelona Connect* (www. barcleonaconnect.com) and *Metropolitan* (www.barcelona-metropolitan.com), which are published monthly in English and are available in bars, restaurants, hotels and many other venues.

Theatres

L'Antic Teatre
Carrer de Verdaguer i Callis 12; tel: 93 315 23 54; www.anticteatre.com
Hidden away with a pleasant bar terrace, L'Antic hosts touring companies and local performers. Expect anything from mime to circus, plus plays and films.

Sala Beckett
Carrer de Ca l'Alegre de Dalt 55; tel: 93 284 53 12; www.salabeckett.com
Inspired by Samuel Beckett, this small theatre is big on challenging performances, promoting Catalan playwrights and works from around the world.

Teatre Lliure
Plaça Margarida Xirgú 1; tel: 93 289 27 70; www.teatrelliure.com
With its own resident company under the direction of the dynamic Àlex Rigola, this theatre has an adventurous programme of theatre and dance.

Teatre Nacional de Catalunya
Plaça de les Arts 1; tel: 93 306 57 00; www.tnc.cat
Supported by the government, all plays here promote the Catalan language. The remit, however, is also to stage dance, opera, music, circus and puppetry.

Music

L'Auditori
Carrer de Lepant 150; tel: 93 247 93 00; www.auditori.cat
Hosting such top-class names as Lang Lang, and with its own prestigious orchestra, this purpose-built venue has a good reputation for classical music.

Gran Teatre del Liceu
La Rambla 51–9; tel: 93 485 99 13 (box office), 93 485 99 00 (info); www.liceu barcelona.cat
Barcelona's opera house is considered one of the world's finest. Top names in opera, plus jazz, big bands and more.

Harlem Jazz Club
Carrer de Comtessa de Sobradiel 8, tel: 93 310 07 55; www.harlemjazz club.es
In the heart of the old town, this intimate space is perfect for nights of jazz, soul and funk. Later in the evening the DJs start spinning their decks.

Jamboree
Plaça Reial 17; tel: 93 319 17 89; www.masimas.com/jamboree

Mika performing at Razzmatazz

Renowned club headlining some of the best names in jazz, open every night with jam sessions on Mondays; also nights with Latin and tropical vibes.

Palau de la Música Catalana

Carrer de St Francesc de Paula 2; tel: 93 295 72 00; www.palaumusica.cat

This wonderful Modernista building houses a beautiful main hall for concerts and recitals. The modern extension has perfect acoustics for chamber music.

Razzmatazz

Carrer de Pamplona 88/Carrer dels Almogàvers 122; tel: 93 320 82 00; www.salarazzmatazz.com

A primary venue for live music, these two locations in Poble Nou comprise five different clubs. All genres of popular music can be enjoyed here.

Los Tarantos

Plaça Reial 17; tel: 93 319 17 89; www.masimas.com/tarantos

Located above Jamboree, this is the oldest flamenco club in Barcelona. You can watch a 30-minute taster show, but check for times beforehand.

Mercat de les Flors

Carrer de Lleida 59; tel: 93 256 26 00; www.mercatflors.cat

Promoting a range of contemporary dance and emerging new talent, this lively venue is located in the old summer flower market building.

Film

Cinema Maldà

Carrer del Pi 5; tel: 93 301 93 50; www.cinemamalda.net

A popular central venue for arthouse and original language version (VO) films with Spanish/Catalan subtitles.

Filmoteca de Catalunya

Plaça Salvador Seguí 1–9; tel: 93 567 10 70; www.filmoteca.cat

In the bohemian El Raval district, this government-funded cinema screens films from around the world. Has a film archive, exhibitions and a café.

Bars and clubs

Hotel Duquesa de Cardona

Passeig de Colom 12; tel: 93 268 90 90; www.hduquesadecardona.com

The roof terrace has one of the best views in the city. In summer it's a great, if somewhat pricey, place for a cocktail.

Marmalade

Carrer de la Riera Alta 4–6; tel: 93 442 39 66; www.marmaladebarcelona.com

This local hotspot in trendy El Raval boasts a 1950s decor, with plush sofas and chrome-backed bar.

Sotavento

Passeig Marítim de la Barceloneta 38: tel 93 221 56 28; www.sotaventobcn.com

One of several lively beach clubs along this stretch (check out Opium Mar at No. 34), which features a lounge dance club on the seafront terrace.

Modernista ceiling, Palau de la Música Catalana

A–Z

A

Admission charges

Most museums have an entry charge, with the usual reductions for children, students and the over-65s. The Articket (€30) allows entry to Barcelona's six main museums for three months (www.articketbcn.org). The Arqueoticket (€14) provides entry to four museums with archaeological collections and is valid for a year (www.barcelonaturisme.com).

C

Children

Children under five go free on public transport but pay full price from five upwards. However, child fares do apply on the Tourist Bus and there are Tourist Cards for children aged 4–13. In museums the age at which children go free, or pay a reduced price, varies. Some larger hotels have childcare services. For babysitters, try Tender Loving Canguros (www.tlcanguros.com).

Climate

Barcelona's mild Mediterranean climate assures sunshine most of the year and freezing temperatures are rare, even in winter. Spring and autumn are the most agreeable seasons. Mid-summer can be hot and humid; at times a thick mist hangs over the city. Average temperatures in winter are 10°C (54°F), and 25°C (75°F) in summer. Nov and Feb–Mar are the wettest months.

Clothing

Barcelonans are generally stylish, and dress codes are informal but elegant. Men are expected to wear jackets in the more up-market restaurants. Jeans are fine for informal spots, but you will not see many local people eating out in shorts and trainers, except at beachside cafés. From November to April you will need a warm jacket or sweater and raincoat. The rest of the year, light summer clothing is in order, with a hat or umbrella in case of showers.

Crime and safety

Be on your guard against pickpockets and bag snatchers (be wary of people offering 'assistance' or becoming suddenly interested in you), especially in the Rambla and Old Town, and at major tourist sights. Try to avoid deserted alleyways. Do not leave luggage unattended; do not carry more money than you need for daily expenses; use the hotel safe for larger sums and valuables; photocopy personal documents and leave the originals in your hotel; wear cameras strapped across your

Dried meat at La Boqueria

body; do not leave valuables on view in a car. The blue-clad, mobile anti-crime squads are out in force on the Rambla and principal thoroughfares. Should you be a crime victim, make a report *(denuncia)* at the nearest police station *(comisaría)* – vital for insurance claims. The main one in the Old Town is at Nou de la Rambla, 76–78, or call the Mossos d'Esquadra (112). From summer 2012 you can report theft at most city hotels.

Customs

Free exchange of non-duty-free items for personal use is permitted between Spain and other EU countries (800 cigarettes, limited amounts of alcohol and perfume). Visitors may bring up to €10,000 into or out of Spain without a declaration. If you intend to bring in and take out larger sums, declare this on arrival and departure.

D

Disabled travellers

The city has many hotels with facilities (see www.barcelona-access.com, or check with the tourist office). Many museums and historic buildings are wheelchair-accessible. The beaches have suitable access, and there are many adapted public toilets. Some bus and metro lines have facilities for disabled travellers (see www.tmb.cat/en/trans-port-accessible). For adapted taxi information, call tel: 93 420 80 88.

For further information contact the Institut Municipal de Persones amb Discapacitat (Carrer de València 344, 08013 Barcelona; tel: 93 413 27 75; www.bcn.cat/imd; Mon–Fri 9am–2pm).

E

Electricity

The standard is 220 volts, but some hotels have 110–120 in the bathrooms as a safety precaution. Check before plugging in any of your appliances.

Power sockets take round, two-pin plugs, so British visitors will need an international adapter. US visitors will also need a transformer, unless they have dual-voltage travel appliances.

Embassies and consulates

Most Western European countries have consulates in Barcelona. All the embassies are in Madrid.

Canada: Plaça de Catalunya 9; tel: 93 270 36 14.

Ireland: Gran Vía Carles III 94; tel: 93 491 50 21.

UK: Avinguda Diagonal 477, 13º; tel. 90 210 93 56.

US: Passeig de la Reina Elisenda de Montcada 23; tel: 93 280 22 27.

Emergencies

General emergencies: 112
Mossos d'Esquadra (Autonomous Catalan Police) 112
Municipal (city) police: 092
Fire: 080

Cathedral interior, Barri Gòtic

Etiquette

Barcelona is a fairly relaxed, informal city, yet it is always worth paying attention to local etiquette. It is respectful to cover up when visiting churches. Shaking hands is a common form of greeting, and physical contact, such as back patting, is a friendly gesture. Air kissing, touching right cheeks first, then the left, comes later. Even when addressing a stranger, the familiar *tú* is used more often than the formal *vosotros*.

G

Gay and lesbian travellers

Barcelona has an active gay community and scores of clubs and nightlife options. Conservative Catholic beliefs still predominate in some sectors, so gay visitors may wish to be discreet. The Eixample district, known as Gaixample, is the area of choice. The gay and lesbian hotline is 900 601 601. The free magazine *Nois* has information and listings of clubs, restaurants and other entertainment options (for downloads). Casal Lambda is a gay cultural centre (Carrer de Verdaguer i Callis 10; tel: 93 319 55 50; www. lambdaweb.org; open from 5pm).

The nearby town of Sitges, just half an hour south of the city on the coast, is a real magnet for gay people, particularly in summer, and is well worth a visit (see page 90).

H

Health

Standards of hygiene are high, and medical care is generally excellent; most doctors speak sufficient English.

It is wise to ease yourself into the climate and food gently. In summer, is it advisable to wear a hat and suncream during the day. You should also avoid any tired-looking tapas, particularly those that are mayonnaise-based, during the hotter months, as these could be a possible source of infection. The water is safe to drink, but can have a strong taste; bottled water is inexpensive.

EU citizens with corresponding health insurance facilities are entitled to medical and hospital treatment under the Spanish social security system – you need a **European Health Insurance Card**, obtainable from post offices or online. However, it is always advisable to take out private medical insurance.

In an emergency, go to the *Urgencias* department of a main hospital:
Hospital de la Santa Creu i Sant Pau: Carrer de Sant Antoni Maria Claret 167; tel: 93 291 90 00 (behind the Sagrada Família).
Hospital Clinic i Provincial: Carrer de Casanova 143; tel: 93 227 54 00.
Hospital de Sant Joan de Déu: Passeig Sant Joan de Déu 2; tel: 93 253 21 00.

For an ambulance, go to an *ambulatorio* (medical centre) or call 061.

La Rambla by night

Pharmacies *(farmàcia)* operate as a first line of defence, as pharmacists can prescribe drugs and are usually adept at making on-the-spot diagnoses. There is always one in each district that stays open all night and on public holidays.

Holidays

Many bars, restaurants and museums close in the afternoon and evening on public holidays and Sundays. August is the annual holiday month, and many businesses, including restaurants, may close down for three or four weeks.

1 Jan: *Año Nuevo* (New Year's Day)
6 Jan: *Epifanía* (Epiphany)
1 May: *Fiesta de Trabajo* (Labour Day)
24 June: *San Juan* (St John's Day)
15 Aug: *Asunción* (Assumption)
11 Sept: *La Diada* (Catalan National Day)
24 Sept: *La Mercè* (Day of Mercedes, Barcelona's patron saint)
1 Nov: *Todos los Santos* (All Saints' Day)
6 Dec: *Día de la Constitución* (Constitution Day)
8 Dec: *Inmaculada Concepció* (Immaculate Conception)
25–26 Dec: *Navidad* (Christmas)
Movable Feasts:
Feb/Mar: *Mardi Gras* (Shrove Tuesday/ Carnival)
Late Mar/Apr: *Viernes Santo* (Good Friday)
Late Mar/Apr: *Lunes de Pascua* (Easter Monday)
Early to mid-June: *Corpus Christi* (Corpus Christi)

Internet

There are numerous places where internet access is cheap and easy but be aware that internet cafés are notorious for going out of business. Try Ciber Virreina (Plaça de la Virreina; Mon–Fri 9am–midnight, Sat–Sun 11am–midnight); inetcorner (Carrer de Sardenya 306; tel: 92 244 80 80; www.inetcorner.net; Mon–Sat 10am–10pm, Sun noon–8pm).

L

Left luggage

Left-luggage lockers *(consigna)* are available in the main railway stations (Sants and Estació de França), at Barcelona Nord bus station, at the sea terminal on Moll de Sant Bertran and at El Prat airport. Or try Locker Barcelona (Carrer Estruc 36; www.lockerbarcelona.com) in the city centre just off Plaça de Catalunya.

Lost property

There is a lost property office at Plaça de Carles Pi i Sunyer 8, close to Plaça de Catalunya; tel: 93 413 20 31; Mon–Fri 9am–2pm.

M

Maps

These are freely distributed by the tourist offices, and often left out for visitors

in hotel rooms. There are also useful local wall maps at all metro stations.

Media

Newspapers: A large number of European newspapers and the Paris-based *International Herald Tribune* are sold on the day of publication at newsstands on La Rambla and the Passeig de Gràcia, as well as in Fnac on Plaça de Catalunya. Principal European and American magazines are also widely available in the city.

Metropolitan, Barcelona's monthly magazine in English, is free and has useful listings. For Spanish speakers, the handy *Guía del Ocio* lists bars, restaurants, and cinema, theatre and concert performances.

Television: The principal Spanish channels are TVE1 and TVE2 (state-owned), and TV3 and TV33, the autonomous Catalan channels. The local channel is BTV. Commercial channels include Antena 3 (general programming), Telecino and Canal Plus (mainly films, for subscribers only).

Money

Currency: The monetary unit of Spain is the euro (abbreviated to €). Notes are issued in denominations of 5, 10, 20, 50, 100, 200 and 500 euros. Coins in circulation are 1, 2, 5, 10, 20 and 50 centimos and 1 and 2 euros.

Currency exchange: Banks and *cajas/ caixes* (savings banks) are usually the best places to exchange currency, as they offer the most competitive rates with no commission. *Casas de cambio* (displaying a *cambio* sign) are convenient in that they open outside banking hours. Those advertising 'no commission' have lower exchange rates so you will in effect pay a hefty commission. Banks and exchange offices pay slightly more for traveller's cheques than for cash. Always take your passport when you go to change money.

Credit cards: These are widely recognised, though smaller businesses tend to prefer cash. Photo identification is usually requested when paying with a card.

Cash machines: These are ubiquitous. With displays in several languages, they will dispense money against your debit or credit card in just the same way that they do at home, using the same PIN.

Traveller's cheques: Hotels, shops, restaurants and travel agencies all cash traveller's cheques, but banks generally give a better rate – you will always need your passport. Cash small amounts at a time, and keep the individual numbers of your cheques separately so they can be replaced quickly if they are lost or stolen.

Opening times

Banks: These generally open Mon–Fri 8.30am–2pm, and also Sat 8.30am–1pm in winter.

Businesses: These open Mon–Fri 8 or 9am–2pm and 4–6 or 7pm. In summer,

A nun in El Raval

many office workers do *horas intensivas* (intensive hours) from 8am–3pm, to enable them to go home earlier.

Museums: Most are open Tue–Sat 10am–8pm, and Sun 10am–2.30pm. The majority close on Monday, but there are exceptions.

Restaurants: Some close one day a week, normally Monday or Sunday.

Shops: The big department and chain stores remain open throughout the day, from 10am–9.30pm, while traditional shops close for lunch in the early afternoon. Usual hours are Mon–Sat 10am–2pm and 4–8.30pm.

Police

The municipal and autonomous Catalan police are efficient and courteous – and generally very responsive to issues involving foreign tourists. In Barcelona, dial 092 for municipal (city) police and 112 for the autonomous Catalan police. The main police station in the Old Town is at Nou de la Rambla 76–8.

Post

The Central Post Office (*correus*) is in Plaça d'Antoni López, at the bottom of Via Laietana, in the vicinity of the port area (tel: 93 486 80 50; Mon–Fri 8.30am–9.30pm, Sat 8.30am–2pm).

Stampscan be purchased at the post office or at a tobacconists – look for the brown and yellow sign that reads 'Tabacs'. Rates are divided into four areas of the world, just like telephone calls: the EU, rest of Europe, the US and Canada, and the rest of the world. Allow about one week for delivery to North America, and 4–5 days to the UK. To speed things up, send a letter *urgente* (express) or *certificado* (registered).

Religion

Roman Catholicism is the religion of Catalonia (and all of Spain) and Mass is said regularly in the churches of Barcelona. There are churches of most major faiths; the tourist information at Plaça de Catalunya has details on religious services, and those in foreign languages. Major ones include:

Anglican: St George's Church; Carrer Horaci 38, off Carrer de Sant Joan de la Salle 41; tel: 93 417 88 67.

Judaism: Synagogue: Carrer de l'Avenir 24; tel: 93 200 85 13.

Islam: Centro Islàmico; Avinguda Meridiana 326; tel: 93 351 49 01.

Smoking

In 2011 Spain introduced even more stringent smoking laws that are now among the strictest in Europe. Lighting up is banned in all public places, including bars and restaurants, on public transport, in offices, shops, schools, hospitals and theatres.

Barceloneta Beach

Sport

Golf: There are many golf courses all over Catalonia: for a full list, see the tourist pages of www.gencat.cat. Weekend fees are usually double the weekday fee. Three courses close to Barcelona are: Real Club de El Prat (tel: 93 728 10 00), Sant Cugat (tel: 93 674 39 08) and Sitges Terramar (tel: 93 894 05 80).

Tennis: ClubVall Parc (tel: 93 212 67 89; 8am–midnight). Quite expensive.

Water sports: Base Nautica de la Mar Bella (tel: 93 221 04 32) has all types of boats for hire by qualified sailors; sailing courses and windsurf hire too.

Spectator sports: Check the daily papers, weekly entertainment guides or magazines such as *El Mundo Deportivo*.

Telephones

Phone Numbers: Spain's country code is 34. Barcelona's local area code, 93, must be dialled before all phone numbers, even for local calls.

Public Phones: You can make direct-dial local, national and international calls from public phone booths in the street. Most operate with coins and cards; international phone credit cards can also be used. Instructions for use are given in several languages in the booths.

You can also make calls at public telephone offices called *locutorios*. These are much quieter than making a call on the street and you pay after you have finished the call. The main post office has phone booths.

International Calls: Dial 00 for an international line + the country code + phone number, omitting any initial zero. The country code for the UK is 44, for the US and Canada it is 1, and for Australia, 61. Calls are cheaper after 10pm on weekdays, after 2pm on Saturday, and all day Sunday.

Dial 1009 for operator assistance for calls within Spain, 1008 for assistance within Europe and North Africa and 1005 for the rest of the world.

Time zones

Spanish time is the same as that in most of Western Europe – Greenwich Mean Time plus one hour. Daylight Savings Time is in effect from the last Sunday in March to the last Sunday in September; clocks go forward one hour in spring and back one hour in autumn, so Spain is generally one hour ahead of London, the same as Paris, and six hours ahead of New York.

Tipping

There are no golden rules. If you feel the need to leave a tip, make it a token rather than an extravagant one. Some restaurants automatically add a service charge to the total, in which case nothing extra is needed. As a yardstick, in restaurants where a charge is not added, it should be around 5–10 percent and about the same in a taxi.

Basketball outside CCCB, in El Raval

In a bar or café, €1–€1.50 is enough, depending on the size of the bill.

Toilets

There are many expressions for toilets: *el serveis* or *lavabos* in Catalan; *aseos*, *servicios* and *WC* ('doobl'-vay') in Castilian. Toilet doors are distinguished by a 'C' for *Caballeros* (gentlemen) or 'S' for *Señoras* (ladies) or by a variety of pictographs. In addition to the well-marked public toilets in main squares and stations, a number of neat coin-operated toilets in portable cabins marked 'WC' are installed around the city. Just about every bar and restaurant has a toilet available for public use. It is considered polite to buy a drink if you drop in to use the conveniences.

Tourist information

The main tourist office is Turisme de Barcelona (Plaça de Catalunya 17; tel: 93 285 38 32; from abroad, tel: 93 285 38 34; www.barcelonaturisme.com; daily 8am–8pm).

The Tourism Information Office in the Ajuntament (Town Hall), Plaça de Sant Jaume, is open Mon–Fri 8.30am–8.30pm, Sat 9am–7pm, Sun and public holidays 9am–2pm.

Informació Turística de Catalunya (Palau Robert, Passeig de Gràcia 107; tel: 93 238 80 91; Mon–Sat 10am–8pm, Sun 10am–2.30pm; www.gencat.cat/palaurobert) gives information about the whole region.

There are also information offices at Sants station (daily 8am–8pm), and the airport (Terminals 1 and 2B; daily 8.30am–8.30pm).

There are also several tourist information booths *(cabines)* located at strategic points throughout the city.

Overseas offices:

Canada: 2 Bloor Street West, Suite 3402, Toronto, Ontario, M4W 3E2; tel: 416 961 3131.

UK: 6th floor, 64 North Row, London W1K 7DE; www.spain.info. Note that this office is open to the public by appointment only (tel: 020 7317 2011).

US: Water Tower Place, Suite 915 East, 845 North Michigan Avenue, Chicago, IL 60611; tel: 312 642 1992.

8383 Wilshire Boulevard, Suite 960, 90211 Beverly Hills, CA 90211; tel: 323 658 7188.

60 East 42nd Street, 53rd floor, New York, NY 10165; tel: 212 265 8822.

1221 Brickell Avenue, Miami, FL 33131; tel: 305 358 1992.

Tours

Guides: Licensed English-speaking guides and interpreters may be arranged through the Barcelona Guide Bureau (tel: 93 315 22 61; www.barcelonaguidebureau.com). Hotels and travel agencies also recommend and advise on guides.

Bus tours: The Barcelona Bus Turístic (www.barcelonabusturistic.cat) offers a tour of 24 city sights with three different routes (Red, Blue and Green), and

Late–night dining, Plaça del Rei

you can get on and off as you please. Red and Blue depart from Plaça de Catalunya and Green (summer only) from Port Olímpic, between 9 and 9.30am daily. There are full timetables at all stops. The complete journey time is about 2 hours on the Red and Blue route and 40 minutes on the Green. Buy tickets on-board or in advance at Turisme de Barcelona (Plaça de Catalunya; tel: 93 285 38 32).

On foot: Barcelona Walking Tours has English-speaking guided tours of the Barri Gòtic daily at 9.30am. Walks (lasting about 2 hours) begin at Turisme de Barcelona (Plaça de Sant Jaume; tel: 93 285 38 32). At 3pm on Tue, Thur and Sat there is also a Picasso tour that starts from Plaça de Catalunya. Walks should be booked in advance at a tourist office.

By bicycle: Barcelona by Bike (tel: 93 268 81 07), Fat Tire Bikes (tel: 93 342 92 75) and Budget Bikes (tel: 93 304 18 85) all offer a range of tours around the city and beyond.

Out of town: Popular tours include visits to Montserrat (the mountain monastery some 50km/30 miles from the city), to Sitges, the Penedès wine region and Dalí country – useful if you do not wish to drive in the region.

Transport

Arrival

By air: Barcelona's airport is linked by regularly scheduled daily non-stop flights from across Europe. Some flights from the US, Canada and New Zealand are direct; others go through Madrid. Flying time from London is about 2 hours; from New York, it takes about 8 hours.

Iberia, the Spanish national airline, covers most countries in shared arrangements with their national carriers (Iberia House, 10 Hammersmith Broadway, London W6 7AL; tel: 08706 090 500; www.iberia.com). They are a member of Opodo (www.opodo.co.uk), the internet online booking service that gives the cheapest deals among a number of carriers. Good low-cost charter airline deals can be found with easyJet and Ryanair.

The international airport, Barcelona El Prat (tel: 93 321 10 10), is 12km (7 miles) south of the city centre at El Prat de Llobregat and has two terminals, T1 and T2 (A,B,C). There are tourist information and hotel reservation booths in both terminals.

The city can also be reached by train or by bus. The national train service, Renfe, runs trains from opposite T2 every half hour, stopping at Estació de Sants, Passeig de Gràcia and Clot, and taking around 20 minutes. The fare is about €3.80. All these stations have metro connections to get you to your final destination.

The Aerobús (www.aerobusbcn. com) departs every 10 minutes from both terminals for Plaça de Catalunya (Mon–Sat 6am–1am; €5.90 single, €10.20 return).

Trams at Glòries

Taxis charge about €30 to the city centre. Agree a fare before you start.

By sea: Barcelona has good sea links to the Balearic Islands and Genoa, Rome and Algiers. Trasmediterránea (Moll Sant Bertran 3; tel: 90 245 46 45; www.trasmediterranea.es) and Balearia (Moll Barcelona; tel: 96 642 87 00; www.balearia.com) operate ferries to the Balearic Islands; the journey takes approximately 8 to 9 hours.

By rail: The Spanish rail network has been greatly modernised. You can take high-speed, sleeper services to Barcelona from several European destinations. The Elipsos Trenhotel arrives at Barcelona's Estació de França from Paris. Progress is ongoing, with a new station at La Sagrera, offering more high-speed links; however construction was held up and the station may not be up and running until 2016 or later.

Renfe, the Spanish national rail network (tel: 90 232 03 20 for international trains; www.renfe.com), honours Inter-Rail and Eurail cards (the latter sold only outside Europe), and offers substantial discounts for people aged under 26 and over 65. There is also a Renfe Youth Card available.

By car: The AP7 motorway leads to Barcelona from France 160km (100 miles) to the north. The AP2 leads to Barcelona from Madrid, Zaragoza and Bilbao. From Valencia or the Costa del Sol, take the E-15 north. Your car should display a nationality sticker.

Within Barcelona

Barcelona has a reliable public transport system (see www.tmb.cat); getting around town is easy, rapid and inexpensive. Get an up-to-date bus and train (*Feve*) timetable from a tourist information office or metro station. An integrated system means that tickets can be used on buses, trams or trains: best to buy a book of 10 (the *T-10*), which works out about the same as buying six single tickets. The Barcelona Card offers unlimited transport around the city plus free or discounted entry to some museums, shows or tours.

By bus: Routes and timetables are clearly marked, and maps are available from the tourist office. If it is your first time in the city, you may have trouble recognising where you are, and most bus drivers speak no English. With the metro, it is easier to identify your stop. But buses are a good way of getting to see more of the city. They run daily 5am–11pm (this can vary according to the route); there are infrequent night buses from 10.40pm–5am. For information on buses tel: 902 075 027.

By metro: There are currently 8 metro lines with two further lines under construction, due for completion in 2015. The metro runs Mon–Thur, Sun and public holidays 5am–midnight, Fri 5am–2am, Sat 24 hours. Good pocket-sized maps are available at metro stations. For information on the metro tel: 902 075 027

Frank Gehry's woven-copper Pez y Esfera

By train: Regional FGC (Ferrocarrils Generalitat de Catalunya) trains supplement the metro with urban lines that travel to Barcelona's upper neighbourhoods – Gràcia, Sarrià, Pedralbes and Tibidabo – and to nearby towns such as Terrassa and Sabadell. Unless you are going to one of these destinations, make sure the train you board (most likely at Plaça de Catalunya) is a metro and not an FGC train – it is easy to confuse them. For information on FGC tel: 900 901 515; www.fgc.cat.

By tram: Trams were reinstated in Barcelona in 2004 as an accessible, ecological alternative to the metro. There are two lines covering six routes, which mostly service the suburbs. For information on trams tel: 900 701 181; www.trambcn.cat.

By bicycle: Barcelona embraces the bike culture and in 2011 was the first city in Spain to install special traffic lights for cyclists. Cycle lanes in the centre are well marked, and the traffic-free port, marinas and beach front are also great for cycling. Bikes can be rented at several outlets, such as Budget Bikes (Plaça de la Llana 3; tel: 93 304 18 85) and from Biciclot (Passeig Marítim de la Barceloneta 33; tel: 93 221 97 78), from where there is easy access to the Parc de la Ciutadella and the waterfront (tandems and child seats available).

Note that the red-and-white bicycles parked at strategic points all over town are unfortunately not for rent. These 'Bicing' bikes are exclusively for resident/long-term use: membership is paid annually, and any use over 30 minutes is charged to a credit card. The idea is to complement the public transport system, to get you to the metro or station and not for touring, so maximum use is two hours.

By taxi: Black and yellow taxis are everywhere and not too expensive. During the day, they are not your best option, as traffic is heavy. At night, especially if you have dined in the Old Town, taxis are the best way to return to your hotel or continue on with the night (have the restaurant call one if you do not feel comfortable waiting on the street). Hail a cab in the street or pick one up where they are lined up (usually outside hotels). A green light and/or a libre (vacant) sign shows when the cab is empty.

Reputable taxi companies include Radiotaxi 033 (tel: 93 303 30 33), Taxi Amic (tel: 93 420 80 88) and Barcelona BCN (tel: 93 113 80 88). Check the fare before you get in; rates are fixed and are displayed in several languages on the window. Also ensure that the meter has been reset when you begin your journey. Refuse a cab if the driver claims the meter is not working. Note that Taxi Amic is particularly geared up to disabled travellers as they have adapted vehicles.

Driving

Car hire (rental): Unless you plan to travel a good deal throughout Catalonia,

there is no need to hire a car.

Major international companies and Spanish companies have offices in the airport and in the city centre. A value-added tax (iva) of 21 percent is added to the total charge, but will have been included if you have pre-paid before arrival (normally the way to obtain the lowest rates). Fully comprehensive insurance is required and should be included in the price; confirm that this is the case. Most companies require you to pay by credit card, or use your card as a deposit/guarantee. You must be over 21 and have had a licence for at least 6 months. A national driver's licence will suffice for EU nationals; others need an international licence.

Drivers must be able, at any time, to produce a passport, a valid driver's licence, registration papers and Green Card international insurance, which comes with a Bail Bond from your insurance company if you are driving your own car.

Rules and regulations: Front and rear seat belts are compulsory. Most fines for traffic offences are payable on the spot. Driving rules are the same as those throughout continental Europe: drive on the right, overtake on the left, give right of way to vehicles coming from the right (unless your road is marked as having priority). Do not drink and drive. The permitted blood-alcohol level is low and penalties stiff.

Speed limits: These are: 120kph (75 mph) on motorways, 100kph (62 mph) on dual carriageways, 90kph (56mph) on main roads, and 50kph (30 mph), or as marked, in urban areas.

Emergencies: In the case of a breakdown or other emergency, tel: 112. On motorways there are SOS boxes.

Parking: Finding a place to park can be extremely difficult. Look for 'blue zones' (denoted by a blue 'P'), which are metered areas; or underground parking garages (also marked with a big blue and white 'P'). Green zones are reserved for residents with permits.

Visas and passports

Visas are needed by non-EU nationals unless their country has a reciprocal agreement with Spain. Full information on passport and visa regulations is available from the Spanish Embassy.

Websites

Barcelona Ajuntament (City Hall): www.bcn.cat

Barcelona on the web: www.aboutbarcelona.com

Barcelona Tourist Information: www.barcelonaturisme.com

Catalonia on the web: www.gencat.cat

Spain on the web: www.tourspain.co.uk

National Tourist Office: www.spain.info

Transport information: www.tmb.cat

Negotiations at La Boqueria

LANGUAGE

Barcelona has long been a bilingual city, despite the efforts of various oppressors to smother Catalan. Franco's was the most recent attempt, but since his death in 1975 the language has gone from strength to strength, overtaking Spanish as the lingua franca of business and education, as well as the language that most *barcelonins* use at home.

General

yes *sí*
no *no*
please *si us plau*
thank you (very much) *(moltes) gràcies*
you're welcome *de res*
excuse me *perdoni*
hello *hola*
good morning *bon dia*
good afternoon *bona tarda*
good evening/night *bona nit*
goodbye *adéu*
How much is it? *Quant val?*
What is your name? *Com es diu?*
OK *d'acord*
My name is… *Em dic…*
Do you speak English? *Parla anglès?*
I am English/American *Sóc anglès (anglesa)/americà/ana*
I don't understand *No ho entenc*
Please speak more slowly *Parli més a poc a poc, sisplau*
Can you help me? *Em pot ajudar?*
I'm looking for… *Estic buscant…*

Where is…? *On és…?*
I'm sorry *Ho sento*
I don't know *No ho sé*
When? *Quan?*
What time is it? *Quina hora és?*
here *aquí*
there *allà*
left *esquerra*
right *dreta*
straight on *tot recte*
far *lluny*
near *a prop*
opposite *al davant*
today *avui*
yesterday *ahir*
tomorrow *demà*
now *ara*
later *més tard/després*
this morning *aquest matí*
this afternoon *aquesta tarda*
tonight *aquesta nit*

Days of the week

Monday *Dilluns*
Tuesday *Dimarts*
Wednesday *Dimecres*
Thursday *Dijous*
Friday *Divendres*
Saturday *Dissabte*
Sunday *Diumenge*

On arrival

I want to get off at… *Voldria baixar a…*
Is there a bus to…? *Hi ha un autobús cap a…?*

Chatting in Park Güell

Which line do I take for…? *Quina línia agafo per…?*
airport *l'aeroport*
railway station *l'estació de tren*
bus station *l'estació d'autobusos*
metro stop *la parada de metro*
bus *l'autobús*
bus stop *la parada d'autobús*
platform *l'andana*
ticket *un bitllet*
return ticket *un bitllet de anada i tornada*
toilets *els lavabos/serveis*
I'd like a (single/double) room *Voldria una habitació (individual/doble)*
with shower *amb dutxa*
with bath *amb banyera*
Is breakfast included? *L'esmorzar està inclòs?*

Emergencies

Help! *Auxili!*
Stop! *Pari!*
Where is the nearest telephone? *On és el telèfon més proper?*
Where is the nearest hospital? *On és l'hospital més proper?*
I am sick *Em trobo malament*
I have lost my passport/wallet *He perdut el passaport/la cartera*

Shopping

I'd like to buy… *Voldria comprar…*
How much is it? *Quant val?*
Do you take credit cards? *Es pot pagar amb targeta?*
receipt *el tiquet*
chemist *la farmàcia*

bakery *el forn de pa*
book shop *la llibreria*
department store *els grans magatzems*
market *el mercat*

Sightseeing

tourist information office *oficina de turisme*
free *gratuït*
open *obert*
closed *tancat*
every day *tots els dias*
all day *tot el dia*
to book *reservar*
town map *el plànol*
road map *el mapa de carreteres*

Eating out

breakfast *l'esmorzar*
lunch *el dinar*
dinner *el sopar*
meal *el menjar*
first course *el primer plat*
main course *el segon plat*
dessert *les postres*
set menu *el menú del dia*
wine list *la carta de vins*
red wine *vi negre*
white wine *vi blanc*
the bill *el compte*
fork *la forquilla*
knife *el ganivet*
spoon *la cullera*
plate *el plat*
glass *la copa* (for wine), *el vas* (for water)
I am a vegetarian *Sóc vegetarià/ana*
I'd like to order *Voldria demanar*
Enjoy your meal! *Bon profit!*

Woody Allen shooting Vicky Cristina Barcelona

BOOKS AND FILM

Books

It is a shame that the books most people have heard of that document the history and culture of Barcelona and her people, are often written by foreigners. The city has a rich tradition of great writers, poets and playwrights, and at the turn of the 20th century it was as much an intellectual hothouse as Paris. At its peak in the 1950s the majority of Catalan writers, like Eduardo Mendoza, Manuel Vásquez Montalbán and Luis Goytisolo, were vehemently anti-Franco and fought hard to forge their own autonomy in terms of literature, yet even they were forced to write in Spanish under the Franco regime.

Sadly English translations of Catalan works of literature are few, and are difficult to find in Barcelona.

The Angel's Game, by Carlos Ruiz Zafón. Set in 1920s Barcelona, this thriller will please Zafón's many fans.

Barcelona, by Robert Hughes. Describes the city's development in relation to the rest of Catalonia, Spain and Europe. Good on Gaudí and *modernisme*.

Barcelona: A Guide to Recent Architecture, by Suzanna Strum. A look at some of the city's stunning buildings.

Barcelona the Great Enchantress, by Robert Hughes. A shorter version of his earlier work (see above); particularly good on architecture.

Barcelonas, by Manuel Vázquez Montalbán. Chatty book covering culture, design, history and some of the city's personalities.

Catalan Cuisine, by Colman Andrews. Describes the unique aspects of Catalan cooking; good recipes.

The Cathedral of the Sea, by Ildefonso Falcones. A novel woven around the construction of Santa Maria del Mar in medieval Barcelona.

The City of Marvels (La Ciudad de los Prodigios), by Eduardo Mendoza. Novel about an unscrupulous young man determined to succeed in Barcelona.

Forbidden Territory, by Juan Goytisolo. Autobiography by one of Spain's most important writers.

Laie bookshop

Cecilia Roth in Pedro Almodóvar's All about my mother

Gaudí: A Biography, by Gijs van Hensbergen. For anyone who wants to delve deeper into the life of Barcelona's extraordinary architect, written by a Gaudí expert.

Homage to Barcelona, by Colm Toíbín. An interesting, personal view from this Irish novelist who once lived in Barcelona.

Homage to Catalonia, by George Orwell. Famous account of the author's experiences in the Spanish Civil War.

No Word from Gurb, by Eduardo Mendoza. Entertaining novel by one of Spain's best contemporary writers about an extraterrestrial who has disappeared in the backstreets of Barcelona.

Saving Picasso, by Mark Skeet. A pacey spy novel set in a fictional 1940s Barcelona where the Communists won the Civil War and Franco is dead.

The Shadow of the Wind, by Carlos Ruiz Zafón; translation by Lucia Graves. Read the novel set in Barcelona then discover its places in a walking tour.

The Time of the Doves, by Mercè Rodoreda. Translation of the classic Catalan novel *La Plaça del Diamant* set in the Spanish Civil War. Visit the eponymous square in Gràcia where the novel took place.

Film

Since Salvador Dalí and Luís Buñuel wrote, directed and starred in *Un Chien Andalou* in 1929, Spanish cinema has had an impact and verve seemingly out of all proportion to the size of its output.

Spaniards are keen filmgoers, and the popularity of cities such as Barcelona and Madrid as filmsets serves as a constant reminder of the production process.

The Catalan capital was smeared with mud for Tom Twyker's *Perfume*, and in 2007 Woody Allen, Scarlett Johansson and Javier Bardem descended on the city to film Allen's *Vicky Cristina Barcelona*, released in 2008 and described as his 'love letter' to the city.

Spanish cinema

The undisputed king of Spanish cinema since the 1980s has been **Pedro Almodóvar**, but other modern directors with celebrated auteur status include **Julio Medem** (*Cows*, *Lovers of the Arctic Circle*, *Sex and Lucía*, *The Basque Ball*); **Alejandro Amenábar** (*Open Your Eyes*, *The Sea Inside*), and **Bigas Luna** (*Jamón, Jamón*).

Recently many Spanish directors have been increasing their potential audiences by making films in English and using internationally known actors, a trend that became popular after Amenábar cast Nicole Kidman in *The Others* and produced it in English. Catalan director Isabel Coixet has worked with Sarah Polley, Tim Robbins and Amanda Plummer in films such as *My Life Without Me* and *The Secret Life of Words*, and more recently Álex de la Iglesia directed Elijah Wood and John Hurt in *The Oxford Murders*.

ABOUT THIS BOOK

This *Explore Guide* has been produced by the editors of Insight Guides, whose books have set the standard for visual travel guides since 1970. With top-quality photography and authoritative recommendations, these guidebooks bring you the very best routes and itineraries in the world's most exciting destinations.

BEST ROUTES

The routes in the book provide something to suit all budgets, tastes and trip lengths. As well as covering the destination's many classic attractions, the itineraries track lesser-known sights, and there are also excursions for those who want to extend their visit outside the city. The routes embrace a range of interests, so whether you are an art fan, a gourmet, a history buff or have kids to entertain, you will find an option to suit.

We recommend reading the whole of a route before setting out. This should help you to familiarise yourself with it and enable you to plan where to stop for refreshments – options are shown in the 'Food and Drink' box at the end of each tour.

For our pick of the tours by theme, consult Recommended Routes for… (see pages 4 – 5).

INTRODUCTION

The routes are set in context by this introductory section, giving an overview of the destination to set the scene, plus background information on food and drink, shopping and more, while a succinct history timeline highlights the key events over the centuries.

DIRECTORY

Also supporting the routes is a Directory chapter, with a clearly organised A–Z of practical information, our pick of where to stay while you are there and select restaurant listings; these eateries complement the more low-key cafés and restaurants that feature within the routes and are intended to offer a wider choice for evening dining. Also included here are some nightlife listings, plus a handy language guide and our recommendations for books and films about the destination.

ABOUT THE AUTHORS

This book draws from original content by Roger Williams, who came to know and love Barcelona during frequent visits to the city from his home on the Costa Brava. He is continually delighted by its contradictions and describes it as a city that is at once one of the most bourgeois in the world and also one of the most avant-garde. Thanks also go to Jackie Staddon and Hilary Weston.

CONTACT THE EDITORS

We hope you find this Explore Guide useful, interesting and a pleasure to read. If you have any questions or feedback on the text, pictures or maps, please do let us know. If you have noticed any errors or outdated facts, or have suggestions for places to include on the routes, we would be delighted to hear from you. Please drop us an email at insight@apaguide.co.uk. Thanks!

CREDITS

Explore Barcelona
Contributors: Roger Williams
Commissioning Editor: Carine Tracanelli
Series Editor: Sarah Clark
Art Editor: Tom Smyth
Map Production: Berndtson and Berndtson, updated by Apa Cartography Department
Production: Tynan Dean and Rebeka Davies

Photo credits: Alamy 120, 136T, 137; Bigstock 9B, 36, 72; Corbis 121; Corrie Wingate/Apa 1, 2/3(all), 4TL, 4MC, 4ML, 4BC, 5T, 5MR, 5MR, 6ML, 6MC, 6ML, 6MR, 6MR, 6/7T, 8, 8/9, 9T, 10L, 10/11, 11B, 11T, 12T, 12B, 12/13, 13L, 14B, 18/19, 23L, 28/29(all), 30, 31, 32, 32/33, 33L, 34, 34/35, 35L, 36/37, 37L, 38, 38/39, 39L, 41L, 42, 43L, 44, 45, 46, 46/47, 47L, 48, 48/49, 50, 52, 52/53, 53L, 54, 54/55, 55L, 56, 56/57, 57L, 58, 58/59, 59L, 60, 60/61, 62, 63, 64, 64/65, 65L, 66, 67, 68/69, 69L, 70, 71L, 72/73, 73L, 74, 75, 76, 76/77, 77L, 78, 78/79, 79L, 80, 80/81, 81L, 86, 87L, 88, 90, 90/91, 91L, 98MR, 98MR, 98/99T, 112, 112/113, 113L, 116, 117, 122, 123, 124, 125, 126, 128, 129, 130, 131, 132, 133, 134, 135; CosmoCaixa 86/87; Dreamstime 24/25, 68, 93; Fotolia 84; Greg Gladman/Apa 5M, 6MC, 14T, 16/17T, 17T, 18, 20, 20/21, 21L, 25L, 42/43, 51L, 84/85, 88/89, 89L, 98MC, 98MC, 110, 114, 115, 136B; Gregory Wrona/Apa 14/15, 15L, 16, 17R, 19L, 22/23, 24, 40, 40/41, 50/51, 61L, 70/71, 82, 83, 85L, 94, 95, 96, 97, 111, 127; H10 Hotels 98ML, 102, 102/103, 103L; Hotel Omm 108/109; iStockphoto 22, 92; Marco Pastori/Park Hotel 104, 105; Mary Evans Picture Library 27; MNAC 26; Núñez i Navarro Hotels 100/101; Olga Planas/Grupo Tragaluz 118, 119; Ronald Stallard/Museu Picasso 49L; Starwood Hotles & Resorts 98ML, 106, 106/107, 107L
Cover credits: Front Cover Main: Parc Guell, *Travel Pictures Ltd;* Front Cover BL: Port Vell Marina, *Getty Images;* Back Cover: both Corrie Wingate/Apa

Printed by CTPS – China

DISTRIBUTION

Worldwide
APA Publications GmbH & Co. Verlag KG (Singapore branch)
7030 Ang Mo Kio Ave 5, 08-65 Northstar @ AMK, Singapore 569880
Email: apasin@signet.com.sg
UK and Ireland
Dorling Kindersley Ltd (a Penguin Company)
80 Strand, London, WC2R 0RL, UK
Email: customerservice@uk.dk.com
US
Ingram Publisher Services
One Ingram Blvd, PO Box 3006, La Vergne, TN 37086-1986
Email: ips@ingramcontent.com
Australia
Universal Publishers
PO Box 307, St. Leonards NSW 1590
Email: sales@universalpublishers.com.au
New Zealand
Brown Knows Publications
11 Artesia Close, Shamrock Park, Auckland, New Zealand 2016
Email: sales@brownknows.co.nz

INDEX

MAP LEGEND

● Start of tour

→ Tour & route direction

❶ Recommended sight

❷ Recommended
restaurant/café

★ Place of interest

❶ Tourist information

Ⓜ Metro station

🔲 FGC station

⚊ Statue/monument

✉ Main post office

🚌 Main bus station

---- Ferry route

▢ Park

▢ Important building

▢ Hotel

▢ Transport hub

▢ Shop / market

▢ Pedestrian area

▢ Urban area